Cambridge E

M000086407

Elements in Organization Theory
edited by
Nelson Phillips
Imperial College London
Royston Greenwood
University of Alberta

OPTIMAL DISTINCTIVENESS

*A New Agenda for the Study
of Competitive Positioning
of Organizations and Markets*

Eric Yanfei Zhao
Indiana University

CAMBRIDGE
UNIVERSITY PRESS

CAMBRIDGE
UNIVERSITY PRESS

University Printing House, Cambridge CB2 8BS, United Kingdom

One Liberty Plaza, 20th Floor, New York, NY 10006, USA

477 Williamstown Road, Port Melbourne, VIC 3207, Australia

314–321, 3rd Floor, Plot 3, Splendor Forum, Jasola District Centre,
New Delhi – 110025, India

103 Penang Road, #05–06/07, Visioncrest Commercial, Singapore 238467

Cambridge University Press is part of the University of Cambridge.

It furthers the University's mission by disseminating knowledge in the pursuit of
education, learning, and research at the highest international levels of excellence.

www.cambridge.org
Information on this title: www.cambridge.org/9781108964876
DOI: 10.1017/9781108990561

First published 2022

A catalogue record for this publication is available from the British Library.

ISBN 978-1-108-96487-6 Paperback
ISSN 2397-947X (online)
ISSN 2514-3859 (print)

Optimal Distinctiveness

A New Agenda for the Study of Competitive Positioning of Organizations and Markets

Elements in Organization Theory

DOI: 10.1017/9781108990561
First published online: March 2022

Eric Yanfei Zhao
Indiana University

Author for correspondence: Eric Yanfei Zhao, ericzhao@indiana.edu

Abstract: Optimal distinctiveness – being both "similar to" and "different from" peers – is an important imperative of organizational life and represents a common research question of organizational scholars across various disciplinary domains such as strategy, organization theory, entrepreneurship, and international business. This Element reviews the historical grounding and recent development of optimal distinctiveness scholarship, based on which an orienting framework is proposed to stress the highly contextualized and dynamic nature of optimal distinctiveness. The orienting framework provides several powerful and unique angles for understanding organizations' competitive positioning in various types of markets, for applying optimal distinctiveness research to different levels of analysis, and for nurturing a more cross-disciplinary and mutually generative conversation on optimal distinctiveness theory.

Keywords: conformity, differentiation, legitimacy, competition, optimal distinctiveness

ISBNs: 9781108964876 (PB), 9781108990561 (OC)
ISSNs: 2397-947X (online), 2514-3859 (print)

Contents

1 Optimal Distinctiveness Theory in Organization Studies

How shall de novo app developers optimally position their products among a large number of rivals in highly competitive platform markets (e.g., Google Play App Store or Apple App Store)? When and to what extent should video game publishers differentiate strategic positions of their new games vis-à-vis those of existing hit games to gain gamer attention and win market competition? How do Airbnb hosts or crowdfunding campaigns narratively position their listings/projects to gain legitimacy and stand out from competing offerings to attract guests or funders? All of these questions point to a central challenge that organizations constantly face – namely, the challenge of being optimally distinct. Indeed, research on optimal distinctiveness has attracted significant scholarly attention and regained momentum in the past few years. Optimal distinctiveness represents a common problem organizations wrestle with as they confront competing pressures to simultaneously be similar to and different from their peers (Deephouse, 1999; Zhao, Fisher, Lounsbury, & Miller, 2017). Conformity (being similar) to normative expectations, industry templates, and/ or categorical prototypes and practices facilitates organizational legitimacy and prevents performance penalties associated with deviance (DiMaggio & Powell, 1983). Differentiation (being different) makes organizations distinctive or unique, thereby enhancing their likelihood of securing advantageous positions and gaining competitive advantage (Barney, 1991; Porter, 1996). To manage these competing pressures, organizations need to understand the conformity versus differentiation tension they confront in different market contexts and engage in strategies to resolve this tension, which in turn shape stakeholder perceptions and organizational outcomes (Zhao et al., 2017; Zuckerman, 2016).

The genesis of optimal distinctiveness research lies in Marilynn Brewer's classic work (1991) on the social self, in which she focused on examining a fundamental tension that individuals face in constructing their social identities: the needs for validation and similarity versus the needs for uniqueness and individuation. Extending this thinking from the individual to the organizational level, Deephouse (1999) was influential in bringing the notion of optimal distinctiveness to the management literature. He proposed strategic balance theory, which "directs attention to intermediate levels of strategic similarity where firms balance the pressures of competition and legitimation" (147). According to strategic balance theory, organizations need to be as different as legitimately possible by implementing an intermediate level of strategic differentiation. Such an intermediate positioning strategy is optimal for balancing the benefits of reduced competition from competitors and the costs of reduced legitimacy, leading to the best performance.

Since then, the study of optimal distinctiveness has advanced in ever-widening circles to encompass a broad set of theoretical lenses, including (but not limited to) organizational identity, strategic management, institutionalism, entrepreneurship, and social evaluations. Reflecting this broad scope, optimal distinctiveness has been studied under an umbrella of terms that include competitive cusp (Porac, Thomas, & Baden-Fuller, 1989), strategic similarity (Deephouse, 1999), competitive conformity (Chen & Hambrick, 1995), strategic conformity (Finkelstein & Hambrick, 1990), legitimate distinctiveness (Navis & Glynn, 2011), and strategic categorization (Durand, Rao, & Monin, 2007; Vergne & Wry, 2014). While not all of these studies invoke the notion of optimal distinctiveness, most share a common interest in understanding and dealing with the tension between conformity and differentiation. A robust stream of research has also been building around this common problem, highlighting how organizational approaches to this tension have important implications for a variety of organizational actions and outcomes, such as resource acquisition (Lounsbury & Glynn, 2001; Taeuscher, Bouncken, & Pesch, 2021; Tracey, Dalpiaz, & Phillips, 2018); corporate governance (Aguilera, Judge, & Terjesen, 2018; Zajac & Westphal, 1994); stakeholder attention and evaluations (Boulongne & Durand, 2021; Gupta, Crilly, & Greckhamer, 2020; Zhang, Wang, & Zhou, 2020; Zhao, Ishihara, Jennings, & Lounsbury, 2018); stock market reactions (Chan, Lee, & Jung, 2021); product ranking and sales (Askin & Mauskapf, 2017; Barlow, Verhaal, & Angus, 2019; Bu, Zhao, Li, & Li, 2022; Zhao et al., 2018); firm reputation (Philippe & Durand, 2011; Rao, 1994); organizational survival, growth, and performance (Deephouse, 1999; Haans, 2019; Jourdan, 2018; Taeuscher & Rothe, 2021); and category emergence, entrenchment, change, and decline (Durand & Khaire, 2017; Durand, Rao, & Monin, 2007; Lo, Fiss, Rhee, & Kennedy, 2020; Navis & Glynn, 2010).

In spite of the remarkably broad influence of optimal distinctiveness scholarship, there have been few concerted attempts to critically review or synthesize this literature. As a result, a coherent body of knowledge has yet to emerge, and more active efforts are needed to guide research and build community around this topic. Several challenges have contributed to the lack of knowledge accumulation in optimal distinctiveness research. First, the proliferation of different labels to describe optimal distinctiveness is a double-edged sword. While it is exciting to see the broad appeal of the common conformity versus differentiation tension, the emergence of so many ways of talking about and studying this tension risks fragmentation of scholarship and threatens potentially fruitful conversations among scholars researching similar issues. Indeed, different approaches to the conformity–differentiation tension may be integrated to form a more general, robust framework (Zuckerman, 2016). Second, mixed and contradictory findings prevail regarding the relationship between position and performance, creating ambiguities in terms of what constitutes an optimal positioning strategy. Third, although Deephouse's (1999) strategic balance theory has had a significant influence on subsequent research, its original prescriptions on optimal distinctiveness are inconsistent: on the one hand, it suggests firms strike a balance between conformity and differentiation; on the other hand, it suggests firms differentiate as much as possible once they cross the legitimacy threshold (McKnight & Zietsman, 2018; Zimmerman & Zeitz, 2002). Partly due to such ambiguity, subsequent citations of this work have tended to be either ceremonial or narrow in their interpretation of the original message by hewing closely to the idea of "balancing" on a singular organizational dimension. In adopting this narrow focus, most studies to date have only scratched the surface of the wealth of approaches and strategies organizations can leverage to optimally position themselves.

Responding to these challenges, Zhao et al. (2017) and Zhao and Glynn (2022) conducted two recent reviews of the literature aiming to synthesize and energize the optimal distinctiveness conversation in organization studies. Specifically, Zhao and colleagues (2017) argued that prior studies of optimal distinctiveness have commonly adopted the presumptions (1) that sameness (or conformity) is equated with institutional pressures for isomorphism, inducing organizational compliance with taken-for-granted cognitive or normative sentiments, and (2) that differentness (or differentiation) is equated with the strategic management push for competitive uniqueness or advantage. However, a key problem inhibiting the development of optimal distinctiveness knowledge is that institutional theory and strategic management have been somewhat polarized in their focus on either conformity or differentiation. Most studies have followed Deephouse's (1999) strategic balance theory and considered conformity and differentiation as two opposing ends of a continuum. As such, organizations are advised to manage these competing pressures by optimizing their positioning on a single organizational dimension and balancing the two pressures as a strict trade-off. The belief is that stakeholders perceive and evaluate organizations based on the degree to which they can balance toward a single, relatively static convergence point.

Zhao and colleagues (2017) challenged this narrow interpretation of strategic balance theory and proposed a renewed agenda for understanding optimal distinctiveness. According to this renewed agenda, future research needs to go beyond viewing conformity versus differentiation as a trade-off and should instead view conformity and differentiation as mutually enabling (Durand & Kremp, 2016; Philippe & Durand, 2011). Zuckerman (2016: 189) made a similar point, arguing that "what we call acts of differentiation are properly regarded as acts of conformity on most dimensions of difference used by an audience, with an adjustment on one or two dimensions." By taking this alternative view of the relationship between conformity and differentiation, organizations can effect a synergy between the two rather than manage them as purely competing pressures. To achieve this synergy, organizations can orchestrate multiple interdependent strategic dimensions and can do so in relation to multiple stakeholders across space and time.

This renewed agenda has proved to be generative. A series of follow-up studies building on this agenda have been published in leading management and disciplinary journals, thanks to some collective effort by both junior and senior scholars across various domains (e.g., strategy, organization theory, entrepreneurship, and international business). As such, significant advancements in studying optimal distinctiveness are clearly evident. Not only has there been a burgeoning literature, but also that literature has gained in its sophistication and complication of the optimal distinctiveness puzzle. In general, researchers have investigated the relationship between strategic positioning and performance by examining the underlying legitimacy and competitive pressures, the different sources and strengths of these pressures, and how the sources and strengths of these pressures vary across contexts and over time. At the same time, however, there still seems to be a lack of consensus in optimal distinctiveness research and a lack of an identifiable optimal distinctiveness research community. Three decades after Brewer's (1991) foundational research, our understanding of optimal distinctiveness in organization studies remains incomplete, and many lines of development are still emerging, remaining tentative, and evolving.

1.1 The Objective and Organization of the Element

In this Element, one main goal I aim to achieve is to build on these recent developments and provide a more extensive overview of optimal distinctiveness research in organizational scholarship. My hope is to contribute to the development of a more systematic conversation about optimal distinctiveness in the study of organizations, interorganizational relationships, and broader industry and market dynamics. In doing so, I seek to lay the foundation for a broader and more integrative research agenda on optimal distinctiveness and release its power for stimulating research in various disciplines. Building on and expanding earlier definitions (Zhao et al., 2017; Zhao & Glynn, 2022), I conceptualize optimal distinctiveness not as a static positioning point on a single organizational dimension but as *a dynamic process whereby organizations identify and orchestrate various types of strategic resource and action to reconcile the conformity versus differentiation tension in order to succeed in multilevel and dynamic environments.* This conceptualization of optimal distinctiveness views organizations as complex and multidimensional entities that aptly modify their positioning strategies to address the multiplicity of stakeholder expectations. It encompasses an understanding of the conformity versus differentiation pressures faced by firms in different market contexts; the various strategies firms employ to resolve this tension; how these strategies are informed by the demands and preferences of different types of stakeholder; how stakeholders perceive and evaluate firms' efforts to cope with this tension; and, ultimately, how stakeholder responses affect different performance outcomes.

In light of the objective and the guiding definition of optimal distinctiveness, this Element is organized as follows. In Section 2, I provide an overview of some pioneering work that has served as the historical grounding for subsequent optimal distinctiveness research. In Section 3, I draw on recent developments in the study of optimal distinctiveness in strategic management, organization theory, and related fields to map out an orienting framework that stresses the highly contextualized and dynamic nature of optimal distinctiveness. In Section 4, I discuss how this orienting framework, rooted in organization theory, can breathe new life into the study of some core topics in various disciplines, including strategy, entrepreneurship, and international business. In Section 5, I focus on one particular topic – organizations' competitive positioning – to further elaborate the value of the orienting framework. I use four example settings – Canadian cleantech industry, video games publishing, stock market analysts, and frontal design of passenger cars – to illustrate how the optimal distinctiveness framework provides several powerful and unique angles for understanding organizations' competitive positioning in various types of market. In Section 6, I elevate the study of optimal distinctiveness from organizational to market level, discussing how category emergence and durability can be conceptualized as evolving optimal distinctiveness work. Finally, in Section 7, I conclude the Element with a summary of my core arguments and a call for a more cross-disciplinary and mutually generative conversation on optimal distinctiveness research.

2 The Historical Grounding of Optimal Distinctiveness Research

In this section, I provide a review of some pioneering research that has served as an important foundation for optimal distinctiveness scholarship. In identifying this foundational research, I highlight the roots of optimal distinctiveness research in social psychology (Brewer, 1991) and discuss some important insights from this micro perspective. Next, I show how scholars adopting the macro approach to optimal distinctiveness research have primarily been influenced by strategic balance theory (Deephouse, 1999), anchored at the intersection of strategic management and institutional theory, and have thus lacked a conversation with scholars taking the micro perspective. I also note that the macro perspective has lagged in embracing some important insights from the micro perspective, particularly in terms of the contextual and temporal conceptualization of optimal distinctiveness. This gap served as a motivation for recent reviews by Zhao et al. (2017) and Zhao and Glynn (2022).

2.1 The Micro Perspectives of Optimal Distinctiveness

The genesis of research on optimal distinctiveness lies in Marilynn Brewer's classic work (1991) on individuals' self-construals. According to Brewer (1991), human beings have two fundamental needs that govern the relationship between their self-concept and their membership in social groups. "Social identity," she wrote, speaks to "a fundamental tension between human needs for validation and similarity to others (on the one hand) and a countervailing need for uniqueness and individuation (on the other)" (Brewer, 1991: 477). The first need – validation and similarity – represents a desire for assimilation and inclusion that motivates belonging and immersion in social groups, whereas the second need for uniqueness and individuation drives differentiation from others, which operates in opposition to the need for assimilation. The basic premise of the optimal distinctiveness model is that the two needs are independent and work in opposition to motivate group identification. Individuals then select and activate social identities to the extent that they help to achieve a balance between the two needs in a given social context (Leonardelli, Pickett, & Brewer, 2010).

   The idea that individuals prefer a balance between the two opposing needs of assimilation and differentiation is not novel and is widely accepted in social psychology research. Theories of uniqueness (Fromkin & Snyder, 1980) and individuation (Maslach, 1974; Ziller, 1964) have both examined the motivational drivers of the two needs. Optimal distinctiveness theory differs from these other motivational theories in that individuals pursue group memberships that simultaneously provide a sense of assimilation and a sense of distinctiveness. As such, the balance between inclusion and differentiation is achieved at the group level and through individuals' pursuit of shared distinctiveness (Brewer & Silver, 2000; Stapel & Marx, 2007) by identifying with certain groups. Individuals tend to resist social categorizations that are either too inclusive or too differentiating.

Leonardelli et al. (2010: 66) articulated this idea of optimal group identification nicely:

> As group membership becomes more and more inclusive, the need for inclusion is satisfied but the need for differentiation is activated; conversely, as inclusiveness decreases, the differentiation need is reduced but the need for inclusion is activated. These competing drives hold each other in check, assuring that interests at one level are not consistently sacrificed to interests at the other. According to the model, the two opposing motives produce an emergent characteristic – the capacity for social identification with distinctive groups that satisfy both needs simultaneously.

In other words, optimal identities are those that "satisfy the need for inclusion *within* the in-group and simultaneously serve the need for differentiation through distinctions *between* the in-group and out-group" (Leonardelli et al., 2010: 67). The essence of optimal distinctiveness theory is summarized in the following figure, recreated based on Brewer's (1991) original work.

As depicted in Figure 1, optimal distinctiveness is defined based on four important parameters: the height of the need for assimilation, the height of the need for differentiation, the negative slope of the need for assimilation, and the positive slope of the need for differentiation (Leonardelli et al., 2010). Note that the intercept (zero activation) of the need for differentiation is assumed to be at the point of complete individuation. This is where the need for assimilation is highest. Conversely, the intercept (zero activation) of the need for assimilation

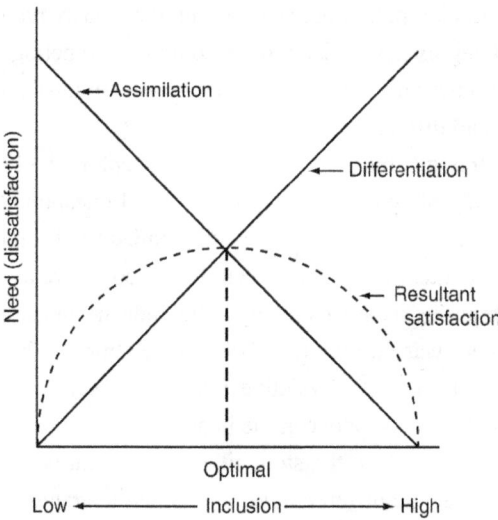

Figure 1 The optimal distinctiveness model: Opposing needs of individuals. Reprinted with permission from Brewer (1991)

is assumed to be at the point of complete inclusion, where the need for differentiation is highest.

Beyond these intercepts, all other parameters are not fixed and are allowed to vary. Both the height and slope of the need for assimilation and of the need for differentiation can change across situations, cultures, and individuals, and they jointly determine the point of equilibrium at which optimal identity is defined (Leonardelli et al., 2010). In other words, optimal distinctiveness is not a fixed, static property of groups or of individuals, but is shaped by the nature and strengths of both assimilation and differentiation needs. This interpretation of Brewer's (1991) original model has significant implications for subsequent optimal distinctiveness research in organization studies, pointing to the importance of attending to contextual contingencies and temporal dynamics when conceptualizing and measuring optimal distinctiveness.

2.2 The Macro Perspectives of Optimal Distinctiveness

2.2.1 Strategic Balance Theory

Extending the logic of optimal distinctiveness to the organizational level, Deephouse (1999) articulated strategic balance theory, which revealed that firms face "a trade-off between conforming and differentiating" and suggested that they should be "as different as legitimately possible" (147). The central proposition of strategic balance theory is that organizations can achieve their best performance by taking an intermediately differentiated position compared to that of their peer organizations. The belief is that intermediate levels of strategic differentiation help organizations simultaneously reduce competition and demonstrate legitimacy. Indeed, organizations' competing needs for legitimacy and differentiation have strong analogies to individuals' opposing needs for assimilation and differentiation.

To test the strategic balance proposition, Deephouse (1999) conducted a longitudinal study of commercial banks in the Minneapolis-St. Paul metropolitan area (the Twin Cities), a highly institutionalized and competitive market. Grounded in this context, Deephouse examined a commercial bank's strategic deviation by comparing its asset strategy to the industry mean for that strategy. He found that there was an inverted U-shaped relationship between this strategic deviation and the banks' relative return on assets (ROA), which was calculated as the difference between the bank's ROA and the average ROA of all Twin Cities' banks. Thus, the strategic balance point occurred at an intermediate level of strategic differentiation on the asset strategy dimension. The argument was that, in a mature and established context such as commercial banks, wherein institutional and competitive forces were both strong, an intermediate level of strategic differentiation represented the optimal position-ing point at which the costs of legitimacy challenges were offset by the benefits of reduced competition.

Deephouse's work suggests that optimal distinctiveness reflects an alignment between two major streams in the management and organizational literatures: institutional theory and strategic management. At the time Deephouse was writing, scholarly interest in institutionalism was growing widely. Provoked by the question "What makes organizations so similar?" (DiMaggio & Powell, 1991), institutionalism afforded a natural affinity for modeling optimal distinc-tiveness's sameness as isomorphism. Deephouse's (1996, 1999) studies con-firmed this by showing that strategic isomorphism helps organizations gain legitimacy. Subsequently, a number of studies extended these observed effects to the symbolic realm and, in particular, to organizational names (Glynn & Abzug, 2002; Smith & Chae, 2016; Verhaal, Khessina, & Dobrev, 2015; Zhao, Ishihara & Lounsbury, 2013), labels (Granqvist, Grodal & Woolley, 2013), stories and narratives (Lounsbury & Glynn, 2001; Martens, Jennings & Jennings, 2007), and other types of symbolic action (Zott & Huy, 2007).

While institutional theory set the stage for the conforming aspects of optimal distinctiveness, strategic management research set the stage for its differentiat-ing aspects. The latter offered a stark counterpoint to the homogenizing forces emphasized by institutionalism, in that it focused on how organizations distin-guish themselves in the market by exploiting what is distinctive, unique, and valuable about them (Barney, 1991). Strategic management scholars argued that to gain competitive advantage, firms implement strategies that build on envir-onmental opportunities, neutralize external threats, and exploit internal strengths (Peteraf & Barney, 2003). They do so by identifying favorable indus-try contexts (Porter, 1980), cultivating unique market positions, and developing resources and capabilities that are valuable, rare, and inimitable by competitors (Barney, 1991; Peteraf, 1993). Moreover, firms can further buttress their uniqueness and distinction and sustain their competitive advantage by ensuring strong internal alignment among key components of their strategies and struc-tures and strong external alignment between the outside environment and their internal structures (Powell, 1992). The result is a uniquely configured activity system that is both robust and hard for competitors to replicate (Miller, 1996).

Therefore, institutional theory and strategic management were initially on separate trajectories in terms of their theoretical focuses, with the former stressing the constraining effects of institutions and the need for conformity and the latter emphasizing environmental and organizational distinctions that lead to competitive advantages. This conceptual bifurcation provided the initial theoretical tension that motivated Deephouse's strategic balance theory, which is quintessential in substantively bridging institutional theory and strategic management research. However, the same conceptual bifurcation also led to a strongly polarized view of conformity versus differentiation and a religious adoption and application of the "balancing" idea in subsequent research on optimal distinctiveness, which has thus ignored some broader and deeper insights hinted at in Deephouse's original work.

2.2.2 Reviews and Challenges of Macro Studies of Optimal Distinctiveness

To more systematically review and evaluate the literature on macro studies of optimal distinctiveness, Zhao et al. (2017) first compiled and evaluated all articles in the Web of Science database that were published in five top management journals (*Academy of Management Journal, Academy of Management Review, Administrative Science Quarterly, Organization Science, and Strategic Management Journal*) before 2015 and cited either Brewer (1991) or Deephouse (1999). Next, they identified all articles published in *Strategic Management Journal* that cited either Meyer and Rowan (1977) or DiMaggio and Powell (1983), two of the most highly cited foundational papers in institutional theory. This two-phase review approach enabled the authors to not just generate a population of studies that were relevant to understanding how organizations wrestle with the dual pressures of conformity and differentiation but to also situate their review in the broader conversation at the intersection of institutional theory and strategic management.

Zhao and colleagues' (2017) article revealed that Deephouse's (1999) strategic balance theory has had a significant influence on macro studies of optimal distinctiveness. However, an increasing number of studies have pointed to several challenges and limitations of strategic balance theory for understanding organizations' optimal positioning strategies. First, strategic balance theory sets up the tension between conformity and differentiation as two polarities – that is, as two extreme positions such that an organization is *either* institutionally conforming *or* strategically differentiating. However, increasing evidence has defied this polarized view of conformity and differentiation and has suggested that the two forces can instead be mutually enabling (Durand & Kremp, 2016; Philippe & Durand, 2011). In other words, under certain circumstances, differentiation may become the norm and thus confer legitimacy (Taeuscher et al., 2021), and conversely, conformity may help decrease information asymmetry (Miller, Indro, Richards, & Chng, 2013), reduce competitive disparity (Gimeno, Hoskisson, Beal, & Wan, 2005), facilitate knowledge and resource spillover (Saxenian, 1994), and thus enhance organizations' competitive positioning. Moreover, conformity through adherence to traditions (Cattani, Dunbar, &

Shapira, 2017) or overplaying conventional features (Durand & Kremp, 2016) may eventually contribute to the perception of being unique and thus constitute an underappreciated differentiation strategy.

Second, research adopting the strategic balance view has generated mixed findings, challenging the idea that a balanced (or intermediate) differentiation position is optimal for organizational performance. A number of studies have found that performance is higher when organizations pursue high or low levels of distinctiveness as compared to when they pursue intermediate levels of distinctiveness (e.g., Cennamo & Santalo, 2013; Jennings, Jennings, & Greenwood, 2009; Zott & Amit, 2007). These mixed findings indicate that there may not be a universally applicable optimal positioning strategy. Rather, what constitutes an optimally distinctive strategy may vary across different contexts.

Third, most studies adopting strategic balance theory have focused on a single organizational dimension in examining organizations' conformity and distinctiveness, while in reality, organizations can leverage multiple organizational dimensions to achieve legitimacy and differentiation simultaneously (Gupta, Crilly, & Greckhamer, 2020; McKnight & Zietsma, 2018).

Fourth, most studies have also assumed that there is a static convergence point that represents the optimal positioning strategy for an organization. However, the relative strengths of legitimacy and competitive pressures do not remain constant but may change over time, thus pushing an organization's optimal positioning strategy one way or the other (Zhao et al., 2018).

Finally, the stakeholders that evaluate and judge optimal distinctiveness are often undertheorized (Zhao et al., 2017; Zuckerman, 1999). Studies in the literature have mainly focused on a single type of stakeholder (e.g., shareholders) and, in most cases, have left stakeholders' preferences and demands in the background (Buhr, Funk, & Owen-Smith, 2021).

These challenges suggest that a broader, and more contextualized, and more dynamic research agenda on optimal distinctiveness is needed. Taking a step toward this agenda, I believe recent developments in both institutional theory and strategic management have provided fodder for going beyond strategic balance theory and developing a more contemporary and enriched understanding of optimal distinctiveness.

2.3 The Broadening Interface between Institutional Theory and Strategic Management

While the early work on institutional theory typically viewed institutions as highly rigid and constraining and documented isomorphism across a variety of settings (Scott, 2001), more recent conceptualizations have redirected attention toward institutional heterogeneity, organizational agency, and environmental complexity (Greenwood, Raynard, Kodeih, Micelotta, & Lounsbury, 2011; Thornton, Ocasio, & Lounsbury, 2012; Wry, Cobb, & Aldrich, 2013). According to these revised conceptualizations, institutional environments are more fragmented, contested, and dynamic, imposing both opportunities and constraints on organizational actions (Durand & Jourdan, 2012; Durand et al., 2007). This conceptual shift has opened up avenues for more fruitful integrations of institutional theory and strategic management, making a more enriched understanding of optimal distinctiveness possible.

Noteworthy in this conceptual shift is the work by Oliver (1991), who advanced an early theoretical integration of the institutional and strategic perspectives by theorizing a range of strategic responses to institutional forces. Her subsequent work (Oliver, 1997) further contributed to this theoretical integration by suggesting that firms' heterogeneity rests on their distinctive portfolios of resource and institutional capital and that their competitive advantage depends on how the use of firm-specific resources is enabled or inhibited by broader industry influences. Later studies followed this approach, pointing to the fact that conformity and differentiation are not necessarily opposing forces. Rather, conformity and the resulting legitimacy can be converted into firm-level institutional capital to enhance differentiation (Suchman, 1995). For example, Rao (1994) portrayed reputation, a distinctive intangible organizational resource, as an outcome of legitimation processes. Analyzing the American auto industry between 1895 and 1912, he found that legitimation processes through certification contests are important for conferring organizations with cognitive validity, creating status hierarchies, and building organizations' reputations.

The development of the institutional logics perspective further fueled the conceptual shift by focusing on how institutional pluralism and complexity offer multiple forms of rationality (Friedland & Alford, 1991; Greenwood et al., 2011; Thornton & Ocasio, 1999; Thornton et al., 2012). According to the institutional logics perspective, society is composed of multiple institutional orders, fields, and markets comprising various constellations of norms and beliefs that differentially shape organizations. These heterogenous institutional environments not only confine organizations' actions but also enable them to more actively and strategically manipulate institutional and cultural resources in their strategic positioning to appeal to different stakeholders (Durand, Szostak, Jourdan, & Thornton, 2013). Thus, the institutional logics perspective goes beyond earlier studies focusing on how actors react to normative pressures (Oliver, 1991) by emphasizing the prevalence of coexisting and sometimes competing institutional norms and stakeholder demands and highlighting how organizations navigate and capitalize on such institutional complexity (Cobb, Wry, & Zhao, 2016; Greenwood et al., 2011; Wry & Zhao, 2018; Zhao & Lounsbury, 2016; Zhao & Wry, 2016).

The growing literature on institutional work also has directed scholars' attention towards "the practices of individual and collective actors aimed at creating, maintaining, and disrupting institutions" and thus has contributed to bringing individuals' agency back into institutional theory (Lawrence & Suddaby, 2006; Lawrence, Suddaby, & Leca, 2011: 52). Such institutional work not only includes those successful instances of "institutional entrepreneurship that produce new structures, practices, or regimes (Garud, Jain, & Kumaraswamy, 2002; Greenwood & Suddaby, 2006; Maguire, Hardy, & Lawrence, 2004), social transformations that spawn new logics (Suddaby & Greenwood, 2005), or the widespread adoption of innovation such that it affects a new normative order or taken-for-granted status quo (Hinings & Greenwood, 1988; Tolbert & Zucker, 1983)," but also includes "myriad, day-to-day equivocal instances of agency that, although aimed at affecting the institutional order, represent a complex mélange of forms of agency – successful and not, simultaneously radical and conservative, strategic and emotional, full of compromises, and rife with unintended consequences" (Lawrence, Suddaby, & Leca, 2011: 52–3).

As such, both the institutional logics perspective and the study of institutional work promulgated a conceptual shift from institutional homogeneity to institutional heterogeneity and brought agency and strategic actions to the fore. This conceptual shift aligns well with recent developments in the study of categorization and cultural entrepreneurship. The literature on categories and categorization has shifted from an early focus on the constraining effects of strong institutionalized categorization schemes (Zuckerman, 1999) to a more recent conceptualization of categories as fluid systems with fuzzy and evolving boundaries (Durand & Paolella, 2013; Rao, Monin, & Durand, 2005; Ruef & Patterson, 2009). Market actors are also no longer viewed simply as passive participants in established market categories but rather as agents who actively influence the creation of categories (Khaire & Wadhwani, 2010), shape their boundaries and relationships (Lounsbury & Rao, 2004; Vergne, 2012), and strategically position within and between categories to gain competitive advantage (Cattani, Ferriani, Negro, & Perretti, 2008; Wry, Lounsbury, & Jennings, 2014; Zhao et al., 2013; Zhao et al., 2018). In addition, there is increasing evidence suggesting that the relative strengths of the constraining and enabling effects of categories are not constant but manifest differently across different audiences (Pontikes, 2012; Zuckerman, 2016) and change as categories evolve (Hsu & Grodal, 2015; Zhao et al., 2018).

Similarly, cultural entrepreneurship research has embraced a more agentic understanding of culture and has focused on examining how actors creatively and strategically assess and deploy various cultural tools (Swidler, 1986) in constructing their identities and conveying entrepreneurial stories in order to gain legitimacy and acquire resources from external stakeholders (Lounsbury & Glynn, 2019). In particular, Lounsbury and Glynn (2001: 552) explicated the role of optimal distinctiveness in enabling entrepreneurial resource acquisition and wealth creation: "[W]e believe that entrepreneurs strive for 'optimal distinctiveness' (Brewer, 1991); that is, to balance the need for strategic distinctiveness against that of normative appropriateness (Glynn & Abzug, 1998) and other industry-level structural factors that may cause organizations to become more homogeneous." They argued that the primary vehicle for achieving and signaling optimal distinctiveness is identity, manifest in an individual's entrepreneurial story, which should balance normative appropriateness against strategic uniqueness. In the same vein, Navis and Glynn (2011: 480) proposed that plausible entrepreneurial identities are legitimately distinctive when "they consist of legitimating claims that align the entrepreneurial endeavor with expectations arising from institutionalized conventions and consist of distinctiveness claims that distance it from such institutionalized conventions in ways that are meaningful."

Scholars studying cultural entrepreneurship have also attended to both the contextual and temporal nature of entrepreneurial stories and identities, highlighting entrepreneurial actors as skilled cultural operatives who tap different types of cultural resource in different situations and adapt their identities over time (Lingo & O'Mahony, 2010; Navis & Glynn, 2010). In their study of two entrepreneurial satellite radio firms, Navis and Glynn (2010) suggested that firms initially cooperatively built the satellite radio market category in their public discourse, fixing and stabilizing the collective identity. With this initial goal accomplished, they began to compete more outwardly, differentiating themselves within the new market space they established. Thus, in the early stages of both the industry and its constituent firms, these entrepreneurial ventures focused first on the collective, with firms claiming their sameness; only later, with the legitimation of the industry, did they individuate their identities.

Overall, across various streams of research in organization theory, there have been some consistent efforts pushing toward an increasing attention on institutional heterogeneity and complexity, a stronger emphasis on the enabling and constraining effects of institutions, and a greater focus on opportunities for organizational strategies and actions, all of which suggest there is a broadening interface between institutional theory and strategic management. This broadening interface offers more avenues for further integrating the two disciplines and serves as an important foundation for developing an enriched agenda on optimal distinctiveness beyond strategic balance theory.

2.4 Synthesis and Renaissance of Optimal Distinctiveness Research in Organization Studies

Building on these recent developments, Zhao et al. (2017) proposed a renewed agenda on optimal distinctiveness that contrasts with strategic balance theory on three key aspects. First, moving beyond the single dimensional focus of strategic balance theory, the renewed agenda argues for a multidimensional conceptualization of optimal distinctiveness. The suggestion here is to examine how organizations can identify and orchestrate a variety of organizational resources to manage and reconcile conformity and differentiation pressures instead of focusing on "balancing" on one single organizational dimension. Second, the renewed agenda acknowledges the contextual nature of optimal distinctiveness and highlights that what constitutes an optimal positioning strategy may vary across settings and may correspond to the heterogeneous demands and preferences of different stakeholders. Third, the renewed agenda departs from a static view and embraces a dynamic conceptualization of optimal distinctiveness. These key differences between the renewed agenda and the strategic balance theory are summarized in Table 1.

Anchoring in Zhao et al. (2017), Zhao and Glynn (2022) wrote an updated review and perspective piece to discern recent developments in optimal distinctiveness scholarship. Specifically, Zhao and Glynn (2022) picked up where Zhao et al. (2017) left off and extended the review by collecting all articles that were published after 2015 in the same five major management journals and that cited either Brewer (1991) or Deephouse (1999). In addition, they tracked all articles in the Web of Science database that cited Zhao et al. (2017), given that it represents a most recent review of contemporary optimal distinctiveness research. Analyzing all articles compiled, the authors found that optimal distinctiveness research has attracted significant scholarly attention in the past few years, indicating that optimal distinctiveness continues to represent a common problem organizations wrestle with. In particular, the authors not only examined basic patterns of citation counts but also engaged in deeper analysis of each article to uncover how the articles have substantively engaged optimal distinctiveness in theory and analysis. The goal was to first understand how recent optimal distinctiveness research is distributed in terms of publishing outlets,

Table 1 Contrasting strategic balance theory and the renewed agenda on optimal distinctiveness

Perspective	*Strategic balance theory*	*A renewed agenda on optimal distinctiveness*
Description	Firms strive to be "as different as legitimately possible" (Deephouse, 1999: 147) by achieving an intermediate level of strategic differentiation	Managing a firm's conformity and differentiation by orchestrating multiple interdependent strategic dimensions in the context of stakeholder multiplicity, organizational lifecycle, and industry evolution
Key assumptions	Firms are evaluated based on the degree to which they can balance towards a single, relatively static convergence point	Firms are evaluated by multiple different stakeholders on multiple strategic dimensions, contingent upon organizational lifecycle stage and industry development trajectory
Strategic orientation	Balance the tradeoff between conformity and differentiation	Effect a synergy between conformity and differentiation
Major precepts	Optimize positioning on a single strategic dimension by balancing	• Orchestration • Stakeholder multiplicity • Managing temporality
Managerial discretion	*Low*: Focused on balancing a single dimension	*High*: Managing and orchestrating multiple strategic dimensions in relation to multiple stakeholders across time and space; using different firm dimensions as levers for conformity and distinctiveness

Note: This table is recreated based on Zhao et al. (2017).

methodologies used, and country coverage. Further, beyond these broad patterns, special attention was paid to how optimal distinctiveness has been theorized and operationalized in empirical studies. To this end, the authors inductively analyzed each article by coding the following elements: (1) the methodological approach of the study (quantitative, qualitative, editorial, review); (2) whether optimal distinctiveness was theorized as an independent variable, dependent variable, or underlying mechanisms/processes; (3) the measurement of optimal distinctiveness; (4) the outcomes predicted if optimal distinctiveness were theorized as an independent variable; (5) the major theoretical frameworks used in framing and theorization; (6) the underlying mechanisms theorized in the paper; and (7) the empirical setting and data sample.

2.4.1 Basic Citation Patterns

The citation data suggest that studies of optimal distinctiveness have been published in a variety of scholarly outlets. These include leading management journals, such as *Academy of Management Journal, Academy of Management Review, Academy of Management Annals, Administrative Science Quarterly, Journal of Management Studies, Organization Science,* and *Strategic Management Journal*; innovation and entrepreneurship journals, such as *Journal of Business Venturing, Entrepreneurship Theory and Practice, Research Policy,* and *Innovation: Organization & Management*; international business journals, such as *Journal of International Business Studies*; and disciplinary journals, such as *American Sociological Review*. This signals that optimal distinctiveness, as a research topic, has broad appeal among various scholarly communities, including strategy, organization theory, entrepreneurship, international business, and sociology.

A deeper look at the different methodological approaches suggests that the majority of these papers studied optimal distinctiveness using quantitative methods. Among these quantitative methods, the most widely used estimation strategy is linear models followed by count models, survival analysis, and structural equation modeling. Most recently, scholars started to engage some more contemporary methods in studying optimal distinctiveness. For example, some employed topic modeling to discover and analyze latent themes underlying large amounts of textual data, and then used those themes to construct a multidimensional space for calculating strategic positioning (e.g., Haans, 2019). Others adopted qualitative comparative analysis (QCA) to capture the notion of configuration and orchestration in optimal distinctiveness research (e.g., Gupta, Crilly, & Greckhamer, 2020; McKnight & Zietsma, 2018). Qualitative studies of optimal distinctiveness primarily used individual or multiple cases, analyzing data gathered from semi-structured interviews and archives (e.g., McDonald & Eisenhardt, 2020; Tracey, Dalpiaz, & Phillips, 2018).

In terms of country coverage, most studies are based on samples of American organizations. A number of scholars have also expanded the empirical scope of optimal distinctiveness research by examining its applicability outside the United States. Studies of Chinese organizations, for instance, are on the rise. The remaining studies examined optimal distinctiveness in a variety of different countries covering Australia, Europe, and South and Southeast Asia.

2.4.2 Theorization of Optimal Distinctiveness and Operationalization of Distinctiveness (or Conformity)

Beyond these general citation patterns, the theorization of optimal distinctiveness in recent studies demonstrates strong connections with other major theoretical frameworks, such as categories, institutional theory, organizational identity, competitive positioning, and market entry. Indeed, most scholars did not use optimal distinctiveness as a standalone framework in formulating and theorizing their papers but instead coupled it with other major theoretical frameworks. Among the wide range of theories used in the literature, categories/categorization, institutional logics and institutional theory more generally, identity/identity work, family business, and cultural entrepreneurship stand out as the most engaged theories in optimal distinctiveness research. This list is not surprising given the theoretical roots of organizational optimal distinctiveness scholarship that I discussed earlier.

Among those articles that reveal how optimal distinctiveness was theorized, the vast majority used distinctiveness (or conformity) as an independent variable to predict certain outcomes. These outcomes are wide ranging and span different levels. For example, some studies examined how distinctiveness (or conformity) contributes to individual-level outcomes such as entrepreneurs' legitimacy building (e.g., Hamid, O'Kane, & Everett, 2019). Others studied how distinctiveness (or conformity) affects organizational-level outcomes such as new venture resource acquisition (e.g., Micelotta, Washington, & Docekalova, 2018), product ranking and sales (e.g., Askin & Mauskapf, 2017; Zhao et al., 2018), stakeholder attention and evaluation (e.g., Zhang et al., 2020; Zhao et al. 2018), and organizational survival and performance (e.g., Haans, 2019; Jourdan, 2018). Still others examined the role of distinctiveness (or conformity) in shaping field-level outcomes such as field emergence and stabilization (Garud, Lant, & Schildt, 2019) and the creation and growth of a new ecosystem (Snihur, Thomas, & Burgelman, 2018). As such, optimal distinctiveness seems to function across different levels (Bu, Zhao, Li, & Li, 2022) and have a prevalent impact on both intermediate (e.g., stakeholder attention, resource acquisition) and ultimate performance (e.g., ROA, Tobin's Q) outcomes.

Other studies have either theorized distinctiveness (or conformity) as a dependent variable and examined its antecedents (e.g., Durand & Kremp, 2016; Prato, Kypraios, Ertug, & Lee, 2019; Semadeni, 2006; Syakhroza, Paolella, & Munir, 2019) or theorized optimal distinctiveness as an underlying mechanism or process (e.g., Tracey et al., 2018). However, such studies remain rare and research to date has largely overlooked why and how organizations pursue certain positioning strategies and achieve a certain level of distinctiveness (or conformity). As a result, "this has left us with a limited understanding of why certain organizations position themselves in the optimal way and others do not" (Durand & Haans, 2021: 2).

Regarding the measurement of distinctiveness (or conformity), studies tend to vary depending on the empirical context. However, one common approach was to create some sort of conformity, typicality, or differentiation index that calculates similarities or distances of a focal organization from category prototypes, industry norms, or exemplary entities as benchmarks. The similarities or distances were normally calculated based on substantive technical features coded on certain strategic dimensions, such as corporate social responsibility practices (e.g., Zhang, Wang, & Zhou, 2020); sonic features and genres (e.g., Askin & Mauskapf, 2017); strategies related to risk, innovation, and operational efficiency (e.g., Miller, Amore, Le Breton-Miller, Minichilli, & Quarato, 2018); and topics derived from large amounts of textual data (e.g., Haans, 2019). This consistency in measurement will help contribute to the replication and accumulation of knowledge in optimal distinctiveness research over time. More recent work on optimal distinctiveness also invited greater precision and nuance in measuring optimal positioning strategies, providing opportunities for scholars to engage contemporary empirical methods, such as QCA, topic modeling, and other types of natural language processing technique. I offer a more detailed discussion of these methodological implications in Section 3.5.

In spite of the heterogeneous empirical contexts covered and the varied measurements used by optimal distinctiveness studies, the mechanisms theorized in these studies that underpin the relationship between strategic positioning and performance seem to be highly consistent. Most studies proposed a baseline relationship between positioning and performance and its various contingencies by examining the underlying legitimacy and competitive pressures, the different sources and strengths of these pressures, and how the sources and strengths of these pressures vary across contexts and over time.

Overall, Zhao and colleagues' (2017) renewed agenda on optimal distinctiveness and propositions for future research directions in terms of contextual contingencies, multidimensionality, and temporal dynamics have proved to be generative and have motivated a series of studies, thanks to the collective efforts of both junior and senior scholars across various domains. Optimal distinctiveness research has regained steam in recent years, and the time is now ripe to offer an orienting framework for guiding future research on this important topic.

3 An Orienting Framework for Macro Research on Optimal Distinctiveness

Building on and extending the recent reviews done by Zhao and colleagues (Zhao et al., 2017; Zhao & Glynn, 2022), I introduce an orienting framework to guide future macro-level research on optimal distinctiveness. The core elements of this orienting framework are depicted in Figure 2, which include: the multidimensionality of optimal distinctiveness, contextual contingencies of optimal distinctiveness, temporal dynamics of optimal distinctiveness, and benchmarks for gauging optimal distinctiveness. These core elements resonate with the definition of optimal distinctiveness I offered in Section 1.1, in which optimal distinctiveness is conceptualized as *a dynamic process whereby organizations identify and orchestrate various types of strategic resource and action to reconcile the conformity versus differentiation tension in order to succeed in multilevel and dynamic environments.* However, these four core elements are not meant to be exhaustive, let alone to dictate scholars' research focus. Instead, the purpose of this orienting framework is to seed ideas and guide future research in a more generative fashion.

In the following sections, I zoom in on each of the core elements comprising this framework and discuss in detail their implications for optimal distinctiveness research. In doing so, I draw on recent studies addressing these elements and use specific examples to illustrate the ideas. In the background of this framework lies the notion of stakeholder multiplicity, i.e., we need to be conscious of the differences in evaluative frameworks of different types of stakeholder in examining the four core elements. I will discuss this issue along with other important boundary conditions of optimal distinctiveness research in further detail in Section 3.6.

3.1 The Multidimensionality of Optimal Distinctiveness and the Paradoxical Relationship Between Conformity and Differentiation

One key element of the orienting framework, as shown in Figure 2, regards the relationship between conformity and differentiation pressures. As discussed

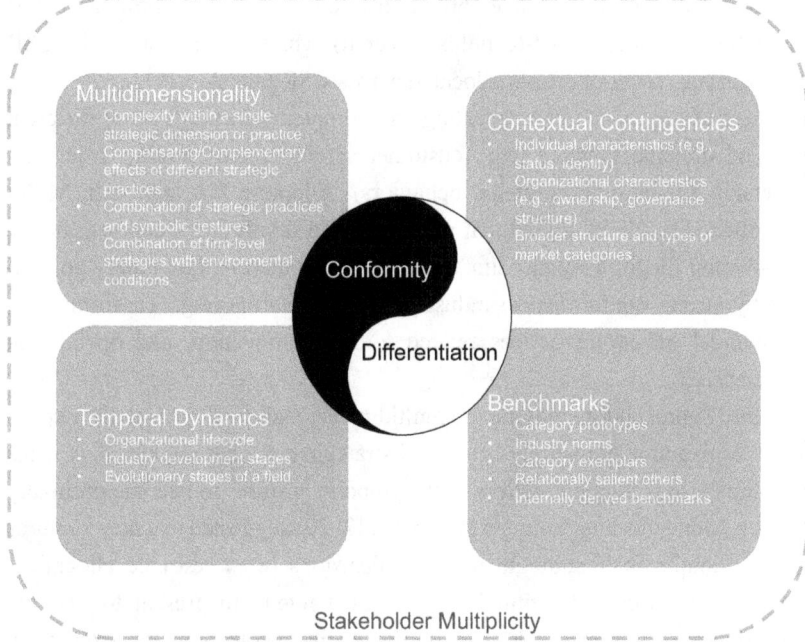

Figure 2 An orienting framework for macro research on optimal distinctiveness

earlier, strategic balance theory views these two pressures as opposing ends on one organizational dimension. To be fair, Deephouse (1999) acknowledged that examining only one organizational dimension (in his case, asset strategy) was a limitation and recommended that future research incorporate other firm attributes into a more generate theory of firm balance. However, this insight has not been taken seriously until Zhao and colleagues' (2017) call for research to go beyond this single dimensional focus in studying optimal distinctiveness and attend to how organizations configure and orchestrate a variety of strategic resources to manage conformity and differentiation pressures. To reflect this call, conformity and differentiation are not conceptualized as opposing polarities but rather as paradoxical and mutually enabling forces.

Scholars recently started to build on this insight, examining how the tension between conformity and differentiation can be managed and resolved by attending to the multidimensionality of optimal distinctiveness. Some proposed that multidimensionality might be studied by unpacking the complexity within a single strategic dimension or practice. In this case, conformity and differentiation can be orchestrated across numerous features within the same practice. A good example of this approach is Zhang and colleagues' (2020) study of corporate social responsibility (CSR) practices in China, in which they proposed that firms can achieve optimal distinctiveness by conforming in CSR scope (i.e., number of CSR fields covered) while differentiating in CSR emphasis (i.e., level of efforts allocated across CSR fields).

Others examined the compensating and complementary effects of different types of strategic practice (e.g., customer service versus product offerings; ownership versus other strategic behaviors). Adopting this approach, Miller and colleagues (2018) argued that publicly listed family firms compensate for the potential illegitimacy discount associated with their unique family governance by strong conformity to industry financial norms (e.g., conforming to prototypical industry practices related to risk, innovation, and operational efficiency).

A third approach for studying the multidimensionality of optimal distinctiveness is to examine not simply firm-level strategic practices but also how firms combine these strategic practices with symbolic gestures to become optimally distinct. Along this line, Younger and Fisher (2020) suggested that new ventures need to couple their strategic resource decisions (e.g., resource allocation, capability development) with the image they intend to present to external stakeholders in order to be optimally distinct compared to exemplary competitors.

The final approach to studying the multidimensionality of optimal distinctiveness is to go beyond firm-level strategic and symbolic practices and examine how organizations can best manage strategies combined with broader environmental conditions. Following this logic, McKnight and Zietsma (2018) employed a QCA approach to theorize and test how new ventures in the Canadian cleantech industry can orchestrate both firm-level strategies (e.g., framing and collaboration strategies) and environmental conditions (e.g., radical technology, presence in international markets) to optimally distinguish themselves from incumbents and enable successful commercialization.

The common theme across these various approaches is the proposition that organizations can pursue differentiation on certain organizational dimensions while simultaneously gaining legitimacy by conforming on others. As such, gaining legitimacy by conforming on certain organizational dimensions can buffer potential illegitimacy discounts due to deviation on other dimensions. In other words, organizations can achieve optimal distinctiveness by spatially separating the locus of conformity versus differentiation imperatives.

Compared to the separating approaches, a small number of recent studies pointed to the fact that differentiation itself may become a norm and thus differentiation legitimates. For example, Taeuscher, Bouncken, and Pesch (2021) challenged the assumption that differentiation necessarily counteracts the attainment of legitimacy and instead proposed that differentiation can become a source of legitimacy. Analyzing 28,425 crowdfunding campaigns across thirty-nine market categories, the authors found that higher levels of differentiation led to superior crowdfunding performance and that the legitimating effect of differentiation intensified under the absence of alternative sources of legitimacy. This finding is important because it suggests that under certain circumstances (e.g., in the crowdfunding setting, where crowdfunders are regarded as novelty-expecting audiences), differentiation may be more congruent with the normative expectations of key audiences. In this case, instead of counteracting the attainment of legitimacy, differentiation legitimates new ventures and enhances their success in obtaining funding.

Conversely, certain approaches to conformity can also become a mark of distinction, enabling organizations to stand out. Durand and Kremp (2016), for instance, highlighted how US symphony orchestras differentiate by exhibiting highly salient and conventional programming choices. Therefore, compared to the normal association of conformity with lack of distinction, conforming selectively by overplaying certain organizational features may actually enable distinctive behavior and introduce novelty. Similarly, Cattani, Dunbar, and Shapira (2017) demonstrated that a successful differentiation strategy may not require a firm to deviate from its current course of action and pursue distant opportunities, but can be achieved through the firm's behavioral consistency in the face of a changing competitive landscape (e.g., Steinway & Sons' adherence to traditional craft manufacturing methods in making pianos).

These recent developments suggest that scholars should move beyond the conceptualization of conformity and differentiation as two opposing pressures and the treatment of them as an either-or choice. Instead, conformity and differentiation can be simultaneously achieved by orchestrating different organizational dimensions, or they can even be mutually enabling (this is why conformity and differentiation are depicted using a yin and yang symbol in Figure 2). To this end, paradox theory offers important insights given its focus on how organizations can attend to and manage multiple divergent demands simultaneously (Smith & Lewis, 2011). According to paradox theory, organizations are rife with tensions, which characterize core activities and elements of organizational life, such as learning (knowledge), belonging (identity/interpersonal relationships), organizing (processes), and performing (goals) (Smith & Lewis, 2011; Smith, Lewis, Jarzabkowski, & Langley, 2017). Instead of treating these tensions as contradictory forces that require contingent separations or temporary synthesis, paradox theory argues that organization should provide continuous and dynamic support for such opposing forces and harness the constant tensions between them (Smith & Besharov, 2019). By acknowledging and positively embracing the opposing forces, organizations can adopt paradoxical thinking, carry out open discussions, and discover hidden links between competing pressures (Luscher & Lewis, 2008). In doing so, opposing forces no longer necessarily entail an either-or type of choice but are instead interpreted and processed through a both-and lens. This will motivate organizations to mindfully explore the dynamic relationships between tensions and pursue complementary and interwoven strategies of acceptance and resolution (Luscher & Lewis, 2008; Smith, Binns, & Tushman, 2010). Paradox theory, as a powerful lens for comprehending and managing organizational tensions, thus has important implications for guiding the conceptualization of the paradoxical relationship between conformity and differentiation and for addressing the multidimensionality of optimal distinctiveness. Going beyond paradox theory, the broader organizational literatures on tensions, competing demands, conflicts, contradictions and dilemmas could potentially provide a range of powerful insights on this front (Farjoun, Smith, Langley, & Tsoukas, 2018).

3.2 The Contextual Contingencies of Optimal Distinctiveness

The second key element of the orienting framework, as shown in Figure 2, comprises the contextual contingencies of optimal distinctiveness. The micro perspective of optimal distinctiveness suggests that contexts affect individuals' needs and that individuals' identity motives vary across individuals, situations, and cultures (Leonardelli et al., 2010). Similarly, what constitutes an organization's optimal positioning strategy also varies across contexts. Indeed, there have been an increasing number of studies focusing on identifying and examining different contextual contingencies that influence the nature and relative strengths of legitimacy and competitive pressures, which in turn shape the relationship between strategic positioning and performance.

The contextual contingencies of optimal distinctiveness range from individual characteristics like status to organizational-level identity, ownership, and governance structures to broader structures and types of market category. For example, some scholars have examined individual actors' decisions to conform to or deviate from conventional practices, arguing that how actors' positions in the status hierarchy (i.e., high, middle, or low) affect their propensity to conform depends on the sense of security they derive from their ascribed status (Prato et al., 2019). Likewise, scholars with an interest in organizational identity have shown that how an organization responds to code-violating practices depends on the code violator's identity as a category insider or outsider (Syakhroza, Paolella, & Munir, 2019). Relatedly, an organization's authentic identity has been suggested to help insulate a deviating organization from demand-side penalties due to legitimacy and commitment concerns (Buhr,

Funk, & Owen-Smith, 2021; Hahl & Ha, 2019; Zuckerman, 2016). Recent studies have also examined stigmatized markets and suggested that such organizations that openly expose and advocate for, rather than conceal, their unique identities can in fact galvanize support and gain legitimacy from skeptical consumers (Khessina, Reis, & Verhaal, 2021).

In addition to such status and identity attributes, scholars have looked at other organizational-level characteristics, particularly those related to ownership and governance structures. Along these lines, studies have shown that family firms, similar to nonfamily firms, are sensitive to conformity pressures and engage in corporate giving. However, family firms are different from nonfamily firms in terms of the stronger attention they give to noneconomic goals and positive family reputation and image, which push them to use higher amounts of corporate giving as a way to distinguish themselves from their nonfamily peers (Ge & Micelotta, 2019). Publicly listed family firms have been shown to face even stronger conformity pressures compared to private family firms and are thus more likely to follow industry financial norms in their strategic configurations (Miller et al., 2018). They do so because conforming to salient strategic practices helps offset the potential illegitimacy discount of investors associated with these firms' unorthodox family ownership and governance (Miller, Le Breton-Miller & Lester, 2013). In countries where the state plays a major role in influential business activities, being a state-owned enterprise (as opposed to a private firm) shapes what constitutes an optimally distinct strategy. Reflecting this, Zhang and colleagues (2020) suggested that firms can simultaneously conform in CSR scope and differentiate in CSR emphasis and that this optimal distinctiveness strategy in CSR practices varies between state-owned enterprises and private firms.

The broader structure and types of market category have also been shown to affect the nature and relative strengths of the legitimacy and competitive pressures faced by organizations and thus their optimal positioning strategies. For example, the distinctiveness of a subordinate category within a basic category may affect an organization's use of the subordinate category membership as a distinction mark. Consistent with this idea, Gehman and Grimes (2017) found that organizations are more likely to promote their B Corp certification (the subordinate category membership) in industries and regions (the basic category) with stronger environmental, social, and governance concerns. Haans (2019) also examined category-level heterogeneity and argued that different market categories differ in their composition. Some market categories are more homogeneous in that firms within one of those categories are highly similar and undifferentiated, clustering around a single position. Other market categories are more heterogeneous, composed of firms with widely varying positions. Haans (2019) theorized that the distinctiveness-performance relationship varies depending on the heterogeneity of the market category and found a U-shaped effect in homogeneous categories and no effect in heterogenous categories.

Market categories can also vary in terms of their density, with some categories populated by more members than other categories. Goldenstein and colleagues (2019) found that being optimally distinct from competitors is more important for new venture survival in categories with higher density. Barlow and colleagues (2019) further suggested that the nature and type of the market shapes the optimal positioning strategy required for market success. In particular, they studied platform markets (e.g., Google Play) and argued that the platform itself bestows a degree of taken-for-grantedness on the products being sold on the platform. As a result, the strategic benefits of aligning with the category prototype (for gaining legitimacy) are minimized in platform markets, whereas the strategic benefits of differentiating from the prototype are amplified. Similarly, Taeuscher and Rothe (2021) argued that by gaining legitimacy through access to high-status complementors, platforms offering massive open online courses (MOOCs) can benefit from (moderately) distinctive positioning.

Overall, increasing evidence points to the fact that there is no such thing as a universally optimal positioning strategy. Rather, what constitutes an optimally distinct position varies depending on a variety of contextual contingencies. Future research should continue to elaborate on the contextualized nature of optimal distinctiveness and identify and examine important contingencies that shape the relative strengths of legitimacy and competitive pressures. One potential direction to pursue is to elevate the focus of inquiry to the field and national institutional levels. For example, while emerging fields might witness sharp contestation between logics and thus intensify the conformity-differentiation tension, more mature fields might have evolved stable priorities between logics and thus conformity and differentiation demands may have worked out a more settled truce (Greenwood et al., 2011). Over the long term, as fields evolve and the associated institutional complexity unfolds, the nature and relative salience and strengths of the conformity and differentiation demands will accordingly change. How does the change of institutional complexity shape the tension between conformity and differentiation experienced within organizations? Under what situations might conformity (in one dimension) and differentiation (in the same or a different dimension) be conflicting, consistent, or even unrelated? These are all important questions to address. More broadly, scholars can extend optimal distinctiveness research to cross-national comparative contexts and examine how crosscultural differences (e.g., national culture emphasizing maintaining independence and uniqueness versus national culture emphasizing interdependence and assimilation) might affect the relative salience of conformity and differentiation demands and in turn shape optimal distinctiveness strategies of individuals and organizations (Zhao & Glynn, 2022).

3.3 The Temporal Dynamics of Optimal Distinctiveness

The third key element of the orienting framework, as shown in Figure 2, is the view of optimal distinctiveness as a dynamic equilibrium. Even within a given context, optimal distinctiveness is not necessarily fixed because conformity and differentiation pressures are subject to temporal influences and thus may change over time (Cattani, Dunbar, & Shapira, 2017). Zhao et al. (2017) proposed that both industry development stage and organizational lifecycle can have an impact on what constitutes an optimally distinct strategy. This proposition has influenced subsequent research, and increasing evidence attests to the temporal dynamics of optimal distinctiveness. For example, some scholars have suggested that organizational age attenuates the relevance of optimal distinctiveness, finding that being optimally distinct from competitors is more important for the survival of newer ventures than for the survival of older ones (e.g., Goldenstein, Hunoldt, & Oertel, 2019). This is because, on the one hand, new ventures, compared to older ventures, have an exceptional need for legitimacy due to the liability of newness (Stinchcombe, 1965). But, on the other hand, they also have a stronger imperative to escape vulnerable, head-to-head competition with established rivals.

In addition to organizational age, broader market category and field evolutionary stage have also been proposed as important temporal contingencies in studying optimal distinctiveness. For example, Zhao and colleagues (2018) analyzed seventy-eight new proto-categories (i.e., emerging but not yet institutionalized market spaces) in the US video game market and found that in the early stage of proto-category emergence, conformity with the exemplar's features is positively associated with new entrants' sales. Exemplars here refer to those highly salient and highly successful games (i.e., category-defining hit games). As a proto-category evolves, however, a moderate level of differentiation becomes optimal for enhancing sales. Snihur and colleagues (2018) also adopted a temporal approach in explaining how new ventures achieve optimal distinctiveness and found that by engaging the sequencing of distinctiveness and leadership frames, new ventures can reduce uncertainty, dislodge powerful incumbents, and ultimately shape new ecosystem evolution. Garud and colleagues (2019) examined the temporal dynamic of optimal distinctiveness at the field level. Specifically, they studied the emergence, collapse, and renewed growth of the "new media" field in New York City that came to be known as "Silicon Alley." They argued that optimal distinctiveness best describes narrative-discursive possibilities and efforts when fields have stabilized, whereas generative imitation and strategic distancing better describe possibilities and efforts during the growth and decline periods, respectively. Generative imitation enables entrepreneurs to gain legitimacy in the growth period of a field by establishing a semiotic relationship between the symbols contained in their narratives, while strategic distancing allows entrepreneurs to disassociate their ventures from stigmatized cultural symbols during field decline.

In general, both organizational lifecycle and the evolutionary stages of fields, industries, and markets matter in driving the temporal dynamics of optimal distinctiveness. However, our understanding of how processes of optimal distinctiveness change over time remains limited. While research has demonstrated the shift from initial collective identity building at the category level to the subsequent strategic differentiation of firms within a category as that category grows and matures (Navis & Glynn, 2010), most studies to date have left unspecified the underlying mechanisms that might precipitate or hinder the shift from conformity to differentiation.

More directly addressing such mechanisms, Zhao et al. (2018) showed that several forces drove the dynamic shift in optimal competitive positioning in the console video game market, which include growing knowledge of the exemplar, increasing satiation among consumers, and intensifying competition among members in the same market space. Compared to these powerful forces that push towards more differentiation over time, other mechanisms may serve to keep conforming pressures strong and delay the transition process. For example, Mathias and colleagues (2018) argued that faced with an incumbent market of mass producers with a strong oppositional collective identity, the smaller craft-based organizations they investigated tended to maintain cohesion and sustain cooperation among themselves, which reduced the salience of differentiation imperatives and delayed their transition from cooperation to competition. Future research should build on these pioneering works to more fully explore the micro foundations of optimal distinctiveness dynamics by explicitly theorizing and modeling the underlying mechanisms that may either accelerate or constrain the dynamic shifts from conforming to differentiating positions (or vice versa).

In addition, most studies to date on the temporal dynamics of optimal distinctiveness have focused on external, objective (clock) time frames (e.g., firm age, industry evolution stages). Few studies have examined how organizations' internal tempo or pacing may shape their optimal positioning strategies.

An organization's internal time pacing regulates the intensity of strategic efforts and decouples an organization from the less controllable changes in the external environment, thus reducing the importance of external stimuli in shaping organizational actions (Brown & Eisenhardt, 1997; Souza, Bayus, & Wagner, 2004). Therefore, attending to organizations' internal temporal dynamics generates a series of research questions that may help extend the boundary of optimal distinctiveness research. For example, will external shifts in legitimacy and competition pressures be equally perceived by organizations with different internal pacing? How should an organization gauge its differentiation strategy both externally (vis-à-vis contemporary offerings by competitors) and internally (vis-à-vis the organization's own offerings in the past)? How would external and internal temporal dynamics jointly shape an organization's iterative positioning strategies of its products? These are all important questions that are yet to be addressed.

3.4 Benchmarks for Gauging Optimal Distinctiveness

The fourth key element of the orienting framework, as shown in Figure 2, is the notion of benchmarks for gauging optimal distinctiveness. Stakeholders evaluate optimal distinctiveness using certain criteria and benchmarks, regardless of whether these criteria and benchmarks are made explicit or not. Most recently, studies have begun to more explicitly theorize on and test benchmarks for gauging optimal distinctiveness. This is an important step since discussions of optimal distinctiveness become vacuous without consideration of the benchmarks against which it is gauged. Moreover, organizations may use different reference points in their positioning strategies, and stakeholders may evaluate these organizations against different benchmarks, further complicating the question of what constitutes an optimally distinctive strategy.

The majority of studies to date have considered category prototypes or industry norms as the default benchmarks against which positioning strategies are evaluated (e.g., Haans, 2019; Miller et al., 2018). Category prototypes refer to the average values of key category attributes commonly associated with category members (Posner & Keele, 1968; Rosch & Mervis, 1975). In a market category in which the prototype is well established and provides a cognitive schema for delineating the appropriate attributes and features that constitute the category's membership (Higgins & Bargh, 1987), organizations are compared to and evaluated against the category prototype and their legitimacy and appeal are gauged by the departure of their features from the centroid of mean values of the category (Posner & Keele, 1968). Atypical organizations – that is, those organizations that deviate from category prototypes – are not readily compared to others and are thus perceived as less legitimate. As a result, atypical organizations normally suffer negative performance consequences (Zuckerman, 1999).

Going beyond the prototype-based model, Zhao and colleagues (2018) introduced the exemplar model into the optimal distinctiveness conversation and proposed that exemplars – highly salient and successful product offerings or organizations – may serve as important, alternative benchmarks for focusing audience attention, anchoring social evaluations, and shaping market outcomes. The exemplar model is particularly suitable for studying emerging and constantly evolving markets where prototypes have yet to form and stabilize. Subsequent research has built on this insight and studied how exemplars serve as important anchor points for new venture image formation (Younger & Fisher, 2020). Further extending this line of research, scholars have started to compare the relative importance of category prototypes and exemplars as alternative benchmarks in shaping optimal positioning strategies (Barlow, Verhaal, & Angus, 2019).

In addition to category prototypes and exemplars, other types of benchmark have also been discussed in recent optimal distinctiveness research. For instance, Garud and colleagues (2019) found that when there is a lack of consensual understanding of field-wide symbols (e.g., in emerging fields), new ventures tend to use other relationally salient ventures and the symbols they offer as points of reference and imitate and differentiate from one another in generative and expansive ways.

Compared to those externally derived benchmarks, such as prototypes, exemplars, and relationally salient others, Conger and colleagues (2018) suggested that instead of being driven by purely external evaluations, optimal distinctiveness might be shaped more by entrepreneurs themselves. In other words, entrepreneurs themselves serve as the audience, and their own expectations and identity-driven self-reflections may balance with external evaluations in shaping what constitutes their firms' optimal distinctiveness points. Similarly, Grimes (2018) examined how the optimal distinctiveness of new ventures or new products might be a joint result of internal (founder identity, psychological ownership of ideas, and original purpose) and external (socially prescribed founder roles and external feedback) forces. Therefore, the different ways entrepreneurs balance their self-concepts with socially prescribed founder roles may lead to different types and degrees of optimal distinctiveness. Zuzul and Tripsas (2020) made a similar point, suggesting that different founder identities (in their case, revolutionary versus discoverer founders) can set off self-reinforcing cycles of firm inertia or flexibility, which affect the degree to which firms can adapt to become optimally distinct as they evolve.

Overall, research that identifies and examines alternative benchmarks represents an important frontier in the study of optimal distinctiveness. Such benchmarks may rely primarily on external standards, such as exemplars or prototypes, or are internally driven standards based on founder identity, purpose, and aspirations. In addition, stakeholders may embrace different theories of value and thus vary in their categorization and evaluation processes, which in turn shape the relevance and salience of these different benchmarks (Durand & Paolella, 2013; Paolella & Durand, 2016; Zhao et al., 2017). While extant research has mostly considered these alternative benchmarks in isolation, future research should seek to address the following questions: When does one benchmark stand out as more relevant than another? How do organizations react to dual or multiple benchmarks? How does the coexistence of multiple salient yet distinct benchmarks affect organizations' optimal positioning strategies? Finally, what are the associated performance implications?

3.5 Methodological Implications of the Orienting Framework

Examining the key elements of the orienting framework discussed above requires scholars to more actively identify and embrace innovative techniques beyond traditional statistical methods. Three methods are worth mentioning here. First, scholars have argued that set-theoretic methods like QCA fit better with configurational approaches than traditional correlational analysis in addressing the joint effects of multiple organizational dimensions (Fiss, 2007; Misangyi et al., 2017; Ragin, 2008). Second, natural language processing (NLP) techniques, in particular topic modeling, have also been introduced to optimal distinctiveness research to refine measurements of strategic similarity/differentiation. Third, machine learning techniques have the potential to generate more prescriptive (than descriptive) insights regarding organizations' optimal positioning strategies. While a detailed discussion of these methods is beyond the scope of this Element, I walk through some of the key ideas and rationales behind the three methods to highlight their value for advancing optimal distinctiveness research. Note that qualitative case studies are also underutilized, yet have great potential in enriching optimal distinctiveness research, particularly for uncovering insights related to in-depth processual understanding of whether and how organizations actively determine and adjust their strategic positioning vis-à-vis those of peers in pursuit of optimal performance. However, qualitative research methods are more established in management scholarship compared to these other methods featured in this section. Therefore, instead of dedicating a separate section on the value of qualitative research method, I will refer to this method wherever relevant in subsequent discussions.

3.5.1 Set-Theoretic Methods and Qualitative Comparative Analysis

Addressing the multidimensionality of optimal distinctiveness pushes scholars to adopt a configurational approach and embrace a systemic and holistic view of organizations. Instead of considering organizational components as isolated or loosely coupled elements, a configurational approach views these components as interconnected and commonly occurring together (Meyer, Tsui, & Hinings, 1993). According to this view, organizations are composed of a constellation of interconnected structures and practices that jointly shape organizational outcomes, such as performance (Delery & Doty, 1996; Fiss, 2007). Configurational approaches have been a central point of discussion in strategic management research, and different typologies of organizational configurations have been proposed to capture the various ways in which an organization achieves an internal fit between its strategy and structure and an external fit with the broader environment (Miles & Snow, 1978; Mintzberg, 1983; Porter, 1980).

A configurational approach has some appealing features from both a theoretical and practical perspective. Theoretically, such an approach points to the numerous causal relationships between strategy, structure, and environment (Child, 1972; McPhee & Poole, 2001) and suggests that organizational performance rests on the intricate relationships between these organizational components (Fiss, 2011; Siggelkow, 2002). Practically, a configurational approach's explicit attention to the multidimensional nature of organizations closely mirrors reality, where organizations function as complex and interdependent entities. These features are particularly germane to the study of optimal distinctiveness.

Despite the theoretical and practical appeal of a configurational approach, an empirical approach that captures the essence of the configurational perspective has been lacking. In modeling the multidimensionality of organizations and relationships between different organizational components, most research to date has resorted to traditional two-way or three-way interaction methods. Indeed, this is the typical empirical strategy that most scholars studying optimal distinctiveness have been engaging. While this approach is useful for examining how organizations can manage and orchestrate two or three organizational dimensions to achieve optimal distinctiveness, it falls short when scholars want to consider more than three organizational dimensions. As soon as the number of variables under consideration goes beyond three, the interaction effects become increasingly difficult to track both conceptually and statistically. Therefore, traditional linear models are ill fitted for capturing the complex causality and nonlinear relationships implied by a configurational approach (Fiss, 2011; Meyer et al., 1993).

In recent years, set-theoretic methods have been introduced to the management literature to address the abovementioned empirical challenges in the study of organizational configurations (Fiss, 2007, 2011). Set-theoretic models differ from conventional variable-based approaches in that they "conceptualize cases as *combinations* of attributes and emphasize that it is these very combinations that give cases their unique nature" (Fiss, 2007: 1181). A better fit with a configurational theoretical approach, this treatment of attribute configurations as different cases allows more rigorous and sophisticated assessments of complex causal relationships among different organizational attributes and their joint effects on relevant outcomes (Ragin, 2000).

QCA is a method that is fundamentally set theoretic and offers an alternative to conventional quantitative methods based on correlational reasoning. QCA is a case-based methodology, in which cases can be individuals, firms, or other types of unit. These cases are understood as configurations of attributes resembling overall types. QCA is focused on comparing such cases to discern relevant attributes that contribute to an outcome of interest. Initially conceived as a small-N approach that accommodates only cases with crisp memberships, QCA have been further developed to handle large-N problems and fuzzy sets (Ragin, 2008). Scholars interested in learning more regarding how to conduct QCA can look into the professional development workshop "Qualitative Comparative Analysis (QCA): A Set-Theoretic Approach for Organizational Configurations" organized at the Annual Academy of Management Conference and the "Southern California QCA Workshop" jointly organized by the University of Southern California and the University of California, Irvine.

Because of its fit with a configurational approach and its ability to handle complex relationships among many organizational attributes, QCA has recently been employed to study optimal distinctiveness. For example, McKnight and Zietsma's (2018) studied Canadian-based cleantech firms and examined how cleantech firms' configurations of six conditions (e.g., differentiating framing, collaborative strategy, radical technology etc.) are related to their successful commercialization. Another example is Gupta and colleagues' (2020) cross-national study of firms' stakeholder engagement strategies. Using fuzzy-set QCA to analyze a dataset of 122 firms across thirteen countries between 2004 and 2011, the authors demonstrated that stakeholder engagement strategies associated with high performance vary according to local institutional context and firm characteristics.

These studies represent important empirical advancements in optimal distinctiveness research. Applying QCA enabled the authors to address the multi-dimensionality of optimal distinctiveness head on, providing supporting evidence for the ideas that there are numerous pathways through which firms can achieve optimal distinctiveness and that different organizational and environmental dimensions can be managed and orchestrated in unique patterns yet contribute to equally optimal performance outcomes.

3.5.2 Natural Language Processing and Topic Modeling

Just as set-theoretic approaches like QCA enable scholars to address the multidimensionality of optimal distinctiveness, recent progress in NLP techniques enables researchers to measure organizations' positioning strategies in a more precise and nuanced manner. NLP techniques focus on training computers to process and analyze large amounts of natural language data; natural language refers to a language humans use to share information with one another, such as English or Mandarin.

One particular type of NLP technique that has gained increasing attention among management scholars is topic modeling. Originating in computer science, topic modeling uses "algorithms to analyze a corpus (a set of textual documents) to generate a representation of the latent topics discussed therein," based on which new theoretical artifacts or theories are derived (Hannigan et al., 2019: 587). According to this definition, topic modeling is not simply a data-processing technique but can be considered an iterative theory-generation process, which includes a number of steps. The first step involves selecting and trimming the text data. Scholars need to decide on the nature and the scope of the text data that need to be collected based on their research questions as well as the common standards applied in traditional sampling in terms of "representativeness, levels of analysis, and temporal considerations" (Hannigan et al., 2019: 592). After relevant texts are collected, they are preprocessed (e.g., sorted, disassembled, and trimmed) using various techniques and rules before they are ready for subsequent analysis. The next step is to use certain algorithms – preprogrammed sets of rules – to reduce the dimensions of the corpus and discover the latent themes of the prepared collection of texts. These latent themes are represented by observable groups of words called "topics." In other words, each document in the corpus can be viewed as constituting a set of topics – topic vectors – and different documents vary in terms of the distribution (weight) of these topics. These topic vectors are further analyzed and interpreted to inductively derive novel theoretical concepts and relationships, extend previous theoretical constructs, or refine existing empirical measures.

Topic modeling has recently been applied in optimal distinctiveness studies, and the primary use of the method in those studies was to refine the strategic similarity/differentiation measurement (e.g., Taeuscher, Zhao, & Lounsbury, 2022). A notable example is Haans's (2019) study, in which the author applied topic modeling to the full set of 69,188 websites in the Dutch creative industry to model firms' positioning. Each firm's strategic positioning in the industry was represented by a unique distribution across the 100 topics that emerged from the analysis of all texts collected from the websites (front pages and pages one click deeper). Distinctiveness was then calculated as the absolute deviation between a firm's weight on a topic and the industry average weight on that topic summed across all 100 topics.

The widespread availability of digitized textual data, coupled with progress in NLP techniques, has made it possible to more completely and precisely delineate the market boundaries within which a firm competes. Organizations' positioning strategies can also be measured more accurately based on their topic representations in a multidimensional space.

3.5.3 Machine Learning and Predictions

Compared to the descriptive nature characterizing most of the management research to date (Bazerman, 2005), the optimal distinctiveness framework has the potential to push management scholars to offer more prescriptive messages to organizations, thus enhancing its relevance and influence not only among scholars but also among practitioners. To bring out the prescriptive power of the optimal distinctiveness framework, I encourage scholars to actively engage machine learning algorithms, which have been suggested as powerful prediction machines in strategic decision making (Agrawal, Goldfarb, & Gans, 2018).

One great example of machine learning algorithms as prediction machines is the Netflix Prize competition. Launched in 2006, Netflix Prize was an open competition held by Netflix, an American technology and media services provider with an online video-streaming service as its primary business. The purpose of the competition was for the competing teams to develop the best collaborative filtering algorithm to predict user ratings of films and thus help the firm better serve its customers by recommending products to them based on their individual preferences and needs. Some of the methods developed by teams who participated in this competition later became cornerstones for further developments in recommender system algorithms. Today, companies such as Amazon, Spotify, and YouTube all use such algorithms to predict their customers' evaluations of a merchandise, movies, music, and videos. Based on these predictions, they choose what product to recommend to a particular user.

While traditional regression models (e.g., ordinary least squares) can be used for prediction purposes, those approaches work best in maximizing the prediction accuracy on the in-sample data by minimizing residuals between observed and predicted values, but they typically perform poorly in predicting out-of-sample observations (Mullainathan & Spiess, 2017). In contrast, machine learning algorithms like recommender systems can address such overfitting problems by employing regularization techniques that penalize model complexity and overfitting on in-sample observations, enable the algorithms to generalize better, and enhance their performance on unseen data. In addition, machine learning algorithms do not require specifying the functional form a priori and they allow more sophisticated nonlinear relationships. To estimate a model that performs well on out-of-sample data, machine learning techniques split in-sample data into training, validation, and testing sets. The training set is used to estimate model parameters (using a cost function, such as residual sum of squares), the validation set is then used to select the best model (e.g., choosing the best regularization term to avoid overfitting), and finally the test set is used to evaluate the predictive performance of the model.

Such machine learning algorithms have important implications for firms' optimal positioning strategies. First, machine learning algorithms acknowledge that audiences (e.g., consumers) are heterogeneous in their preferences and tastes towards certain products and services. Second, given audience heterogeneity, machine learning algorithms aim to accurately predict a particular audience's preference and taste and, based on that prediction make targeted recommendations to that audience. Following this logic, a restaurant on Yelp that focuses on serving authentic Asian food can achieve a higher rating by designing its menu to purposefully attract potential customers who care about authentic Asian food and avoid those who are accustomed to nonauthentic, Americanized Asian food. Similarly, a publicly listed firm can predict stock analysts' coverage and recommendation tendencies and strategically position itself to attract the attention of those analysts who are predicted to have a positive predisposition toward the firm.

Equipped with contemporary machine learning techniques, optimal distinctiveness scholars are well positioned to offer useful and prescriptive guidance in terms of how firms can optimally position themselves in light of stakeholder multiplicity and the importance of stakeholder perceptions and evaluations in shaping firms' ultimate performance.

3.6 Boundary Conditions of the Orienting Framework

3.6.1 The Infinite Dimensionality Problem and Stakeholder Multiplicity

While addressing multidimensionality of optimal distinctiveness extends strategic balance theory and more closely matches organizational reality, this aspect of the orienting framework also requires scholars to be aware of the infinite dimensionality problem. The infinite dimensionality problem is "a well-known problem in both organizational research (e.g., Durand and Paolella, 2013) and cognitive science (e.g., Goldstone, 1994) ... that there are potentially infinite similarities and differences between two entities, and ... any two entities can be arbitrarily similar or dissimilar by changing the criterion of what counts as a relevant attribute" (Cattani et al., 2017: 66).

The infinite dimensionality problem is further complicated by stakeholder multiplicity (or what organization theorists call audience heterogeneity). Stakeholder multiplicity refers to not only the sheer number of stakeholder groups but also the different interpretive and evaluative frames of these groups (Zhao et al., 2017). Organizations are subject to evaluations of various types of stakeholder (e.g., the nation-state, suppliers, consumers, investors, the media etc.), and these stakeholders engage different criteria in evaluating organizations and their actions and confer different types of legitimacy (e.g., regulatory, pragmatic, moral, and cultural cognitive) which are not necessarily consistent with each other (Deephouse, Bundy, Tost, & Suchman, 2017). In other words, different stakeholders may have different expectations and categorical definitions (Durand & Paolella, 2013), implying not all stakeholders are devoting equal attention or value on the same organizational dimensions and thus no single frame of reference is sufficient to gauge and evaluate an organization's optimal distinctiveness.

Indeed, recent studies have suggested that different stakeholders embrace different categorization schemes, evaluate the same organization through different lenses, and compare the firm with different reference groups (Beuna & Garud, 2007; Bowers, 2015; Pontikes, 2012). The different categorization and evaluation schemes of stakeholders may be due to their differences in prior knowledge and expertise (Murphy & Medin, 1985), their varied goals (Glaser et al., 2019; Paolella & Durand, 2016), or their self-serving motivations (Bowers, 2020; Bowers & Prato, 2019). Understanding these different sources of stakeholder multiplicity helps provide strong justifications of why we consider certain organizational characteristics / dimensions in conceptualizing and analyzing optimal distinctiveness while excluding others. Furthermore, we need to be aware of different situations where one stakeholder's expectation (for conformity or for differentiation) is more important than another's. To this end, insights from stakeholder theory can be useful. For example, different power, legitimacy and urgency of stakeholders may affect the salience of their demands for conformity or differentiation and in turn shape organizations' perception and reconciliation of the conformity–differentiation tension (Mitchell, Agle, & Wood, 1997).

As scholars studying optimal distinctiveness, we need to be aware of the infinite dimensionality problem, offer strong rationale for our conceptual and empirical focus, and keep in mind that categorical boundaries are contingent upon the specific audience constructing them. Accounting for stakeholder multiplicity will also delineate the boundary of our study of the four core elements of the orienting framework (as shown in Figure 2).

3.6.2 Global versus Local Optimization and Different Optimization Trajectories

Most studies to date have assumed that pursuing a globally optimal distinctiveness position represents a common organizational goal. Durand and Haans (2021) recently challenged this assumption, pushing scholars to more seriously address the question "To what extent do organizations optimize their distinctiveness?" for a better understanding of organizations' conscious efforts toward optimal distinctiveness. This proposition requires scholars to conceptualize optimal distinctiveness as a self-selection process and account for such self-selection both theoretically and empirically.

Theoretically, the authors call for "a better quantification of the actual efforts put forth by organizations in optimizing their assets and resources" (Durand & Haans, 2021: 7). In other words, organizations might not actually optimize their distinctiveness per se. Rather, market positioning (optimally distinct or not) might be a result of organizations' efforts to optimize their assets, resources, and strategic processes. Addressing these antecedents of organizations' marketing positioning is thus important for understanding "whether and how organizations actively determine (and adjust) their strategic positioning relative to their peers in the pursuit of optimal performance" (Durand & Haans, 2021: 8). To this end, qualitative research methods can complement quantitative methods in uncovering more in-depth processual insights regarding organizations' intension and motivation in pursuing optimal distinctiveness and the extent to which they are pursuing a global optimal distinctiveness or otherwise settling with some local optima due to limitations and constraints organizations face given their resource endowments, competitive conditions, and path dependent trajectories (Durand & Haans, 2021).

Empirically, Durand and Haans (2021) push scholars to more explicitly model distinctiveness as a potentially self-selected or endogenous strategy. Without accounting for the potential endogeneity of organizations' positioning strategy due to self-selection, most past studies focusing on the relationship between positioning and performance might have been misspecified and led to questionable conclusions. The authors encourage scholars who study optimal distinctiveness to embrace recent methodological advances made in strategic management, "such as the use of instrumental variables in applying

Heckman corrections (Hamilton & Nickerson, 2003; Wolfolds & Siegel, 2019), utilizing field experiments (Chatterji, Findley, Jensen, Meier, & Nielson, 2016), or applying matching approaches on observable characteristics (e.g., DesJardine & Durand, 2020). These more advanced methods would assuage some concerns with prior studies, help replicate prior findings, and support better the theory of optimal distinctiveness" (Durand & Haans, 2021: 9).

To come full circle, I began this section by developing an orienting framework for guiding macro studies of optimal distinctiveness. This orienting framework points to four frontiers that scholars can engage in to further advance the optimal distinctiveness conversation in organization studies. In addition to providing scholars with an updated understanding of contemporary optimal distinctiveness research and pointing to future research directions, the orienting conceptual framework also compels researchers to identify and embrace an enhanced empirical toolkit in addressing new research questions implied by the framework. I highlighted three types of method meriting further attention, including set-theoretic methods, NLP, and machine learning. Finally, I discussed several boundary conditions of the orienting framework and suggested directions for further clarifying and extending the boundary of optimal distinctiveness research.

In the next sections, I build on the orienting conceptual framework and discuss briefly its implications for several major research streams, including strategic management, entrepreneurship, and international business. The purpose is to expand the scope of optimal distinctiveness research beyond its home domain – organization theory – and highlight its value in breathing new insights into other major areas of management scholarship. After demonstrating the broad appeal of the orienting framework, I then zoom in on a particular research topic – the competitive positioning of organizations – and use specific empirical examples to drive home the idea that optimal distinctiveness offers a unique approach to understanding organizations' competitive positioning in a variety of markets, which entails both novel conceptual and empirical solutions.

4 Expanding the Scope: How the Optimal Distinctiveness Framework Can Bring New Insights into Multiple Research Streams

4.1 The Implications of the Orienting Framework for Strategic Management Research

Zhao et al. (2017) offered detailed discussions of how a renewed agenda on optimal distinctiveness can inform studies on a number of core strategic management topics. These topics include: (1) organizational ambidexterity, or a firm's ability to simultaneously manage a variety of paradoxical trade-offs (Birkinshaw & Gupta, 2013; Simsek, 2009; Tushman & O'Reilly, 1996); (2) competitive advantage of incumbents versus new entrants in industry evolution studies (Klepper & Simons, 2000; Madsen & Walker, 2015); (3) product-market scope and value chain decisions (Capron & Mitchell, 2012; Khanna & Palepu, 2000); and (4) market entry strategies, for which a core dilemma revolves around the decision to imitate versus pursue more novel innovations (Lieberman & Asaba, 2006). To avoid repetition, I will not repeat those discussions here, but refer readers to Zhao and colleagues' 2017 *Strategic Management Journal* article.

Zhao et al. (2017) provided several general research questions that could guide future research on each of these core strategic management topics. In addition, the article also contains some substantive suggestions that can lead to empirical investigations. For instance, in discussing the implications of the optimal distinctiveness framework for studies on market entry strategies, the authors wrote the following:

> A focus on managing temporality is well suited to resolve some ambiguity around an optimal positioning strategy. In the context of fashion markets, for instance, our approach suggests that in different stages of fashion evolution, strategic differentiation may take different forms and degrees in order for entrants to achieve competitive advantage. As an example, the US console video game industry is recognized for its multiple, rapidly evolving categories triggered by innovative games with novel feature combinations (Aoyama & Izushi, 2003; Mollick, 2012). These categories build on technological advances in hardware and software, and are propelled by gamers' fast-changing tastes (Bayus and Shankar, 2003; Clements & Ohashi, 2005). Despite the market success and popularity of category defining games, such as Medal of Honor and Grand Theft Auto, the features of such games might not be fully and completely institutionalized. Instead, we observe boom and bust cycles, as new hit game categories emerge and eclipse older ones. For new entrants to be optimally distinct, they need to closely follow a category defining game when it emerges, copy its core features that gamers value, then increasingly differentiate as more new entrants crowd into the same space, and perhaps ultimately exit the market when the popularity of a category wanes. (Zhao et al., 2017: 106–7).

This suggestion not only points to a potential research question, but also offers guidance in developing hypotheses regarding optimal positioning strategies across different stages of market evolution as well as provides a specific empirical context for testing these hypotheses. The ideas seeded in this suggestion have come to fruition. Zhao et al. (2018) subsequently picked up on these ideas and examined the contingent effectiveness of various positioning strategies in new product markets characterized by temporally shifting legitimacy and differentiation expectations using the US console video game industry as the empirical context (also see Zhao, Ishihara, & Jennings, 2020). Similar efforts are needed to address other research questions proposed by Zhao et al. (2017), which are worth further theoretical elaboration and empirical investigation. To go beyond Zhao et al. (2017), in Section 5 I will revisit the implications of optimal distinctiveness for strategic management research by providing more concrete examples of how the orienting framework can inform the study of one central strategic management topic – the competitive positioning of organizations.

4.2 The Implications of the Orienting Framework for Entrepreneurship Research

Gaining legitimacy and acquiring resources are among the central challenges that entrepreneurs face (Lounsbury & Glynn, 2001; Nason & Wiklund, 2018). Most new ventures suffer from the liability of newness (Stinchcombe, 1965) in that they lack reliable operations to establish products or services, need to develop organizational roles and routines, and are still building competencies, so they do not have a proven record of performance or reputation. Because of these challenges, resource providers normally feel reluctant to commit precious resources to new ventures, and this reluctance is further exacerbated when there is a strong information asymmetry between entrepreneurs and resource providers regarding the intrinsic quality of new ventures (Amit, Brander, & Zott, 1998). To overcome these resource challenges, some entrepreneurs creatively (re)interpret, (re)combine, (re)purpose, and (re)deploy resources at hand to launch their ventures (Baker & Nelson, 2005; Sonenshein, 2014). However, such creativity has its own limit and most entrepreneurs, at some point during their ventures' development, will need to acquire resources from external stakeholders (through equity financing, venture capital, angel investing or crowdfunding) to further grow and sustain their operations.

To convince external resource providers that they are worthy of support, new ventures need to present themselves as optimally distinct – that is, they must be perceived as a legitimate enough to access resources yet distinct enough to gain competitive advantage (Lounsbury & Glynn, 2019; Zhao et al., 2017). This optimal distinctiveness imperative is prevalent across different market contexts but may manifest particularly strongly in emergent markets. Emergent markets are neither mature nor nascent but rather in an emergent phase (Lambkin & Day, 1989). Such markets are unique, differing from mature markets in that their boundaries are in flux, their norms and rules are still being established, and mutual understanding regarding what constitutes a prototypical member and the associated prevailing features is still forming. Emergent markets also differ from nascent markets in that the initial contours of emergent markets have started to form, and some pioneering firms have emerged to become the primary referents for other entrants (McDonald & Eisenhardt, 2020; Zhao et al., 2018). These pioneering firms serve as exemplars that form initial conceptualizations of these markets' business and value propositions and provide important benchmarks that both internal and external stakeholders (e.g., employees, consumers, partners, and analysts) use when making sense of the markets (Rosa, Porac, Runser-Spanjol, & Saxon, 1999; Santos & Eisenhardt, 2009).

While optimal distinctiveness is relevant for new ventures entering all kinds of market (Lounsbury & Glynn, 2001; Martens, Jennings, & Jennings, 2007), the imperative of being optimally distinct is particularly strong in emergent markets for two reasons. First, exemplars' market successes not only highlight what is possible in the emergent market space but also delineates certain core attributes of the exemplars and their products/services that consumers value. Therefore, these attributes define what is perceived as legitimate and appealing and thus pressure new ventures to conform to those attributes. Second, exemplars are also formidable competitors. Given their early success and influence, they command the greatest resources from the emergent market space; attract the most attention from resource providers; and, in a lot of ways, dictate the norms and rules forming in the market (Santos & Eisenhardt, 2009; Suarez & Lanzolla, 2007). Simply conforming to the exemplars will put new ventures at a disadvantage because they will be compared to highly successful peers yet have nothing unique to stand out. Therefore, new ventures entering emergent markets must wrestle with the optimal distinctiveness challenge in that, on the one hand, they need to sufficiently emulate the exemplars to be considered legitimate and perceived as part of the emergent market, but, on the other hand, they need to distinguish themselves from the exemplars to compete for customers and attract resources.

Although optimal distinctiveness represents a central conundrum new ventures face in emergent markets, our understanding of how new ventures resolve this conundrum is limited. A number of questions remain unaddressed, which provides avenues for future research: What strategic decisions are most relevant to new ventures entering an emergent market? How should new ventures strategically position themselves in light of these decisions to successfully enter and compete in an emergent market space? How do these decisions relate to one another for an entrant to construct an optimally distinct strategy vis-à-vis the exemplars?

To address these questions, various elements of the orienting conceptual framework of optimal distinctiveness proposed in Section 3 come into play. For instance, the notion of multidimensionality should push scholars to think about various types of market positioning choice, including both substantive strategies and symbolic actions. Substantive positioning choices may include decisions regarding product price, product scope, and geographic scope (Day, 1981; Porter, 1980, 1996). In addition to these traditional strategic dimensions, new ventures may also pursue market position variations in terms of organizational values (Bansal, 2003), organizational image (Younger & Fisher, 2020), and organizational framing (McKnight & Zietsma, 2018), etc. Collectively, these different organizational dimensions constitute a toolkit that new ventures can manage and mobilize strategically in pursuit of optimal distinctiveness.

New ventures' positioning decisions on each of these dimensions also need to be made using exemplars as benchmarks. Accordingly, future research can explore how new ventures can diverge from or conform to exemplars across these dimensions in an orchestrated manner so they can present an optimally distinct image to key stakeholders. Scholars can further examine how organizations' market-positioning choices and their intended image may both need to be crafted and adapted to appeal to specific types of stakeholder. Taken together, research opportunities abound regarding how substantive market positioning choices, intended image, and stakeholder multiplicity constitute a multifaceted and dynamic strategic toolkit that new entrants can use to maneuver around exemplars when entering an emergent market and subsequently competing therein.

Up to this point, I have argued that exemplars in emergent markets serve as important reference points and benchmarks for new entrants' market positioning strategies. In doing so, I have implicitly assumed that these exemplars are passive observers of new ventures' entry strategies. While this assumption enables parsimonious theorization and tests of new entrants' optimal positioning strategies, it is an incomplete reflection of reality. Instead of being passive observers and static benchmarks, exemplars in emergent markets are typically formidable incumbents, ready to respond to new entrants when a perceived threat is imminent. Therefore, future research should go beyond viewing optimal distinctiveness as a singular firm decision and should start theorizing and modeling the interactive competitive dynamics (Chen & Miller, 2012) between new entrants and exemplars in emergent markets. There are a number of interesting research questions to ask: What market positioning strategies of new entrants are most likely to trigger exemplars' reactions? What determines the number, speed, and strength of exemplars' responses? How do these responses in turn shape new entrants' optimal positioning strategies? What resource profile do new entrants need to have to enable their initial entry as well as ensure their post-entry success (Zhao, Ishihara, & Jennings, 2020)? In addressing these questions, optimal distinctiveness should not be considered a particular state that is relevant only for entrepreneurs and their new ventures on entering a market, but as an ongoing process; this approach strongly matches our definition of optimal distinctiveness.

4.3 The Implications of the Orienting Framework for International Business Research

As discussed in previous sections, macro optimal distinctiveness research emerged at the intersection of strategic management and organization theory (Deephouse, 1999; Zhao et al., 2017), and the notion of optimal distinctiveness has also been considered a central element in the cultural entrepreneurship literature (Lounsbury & Glynn, 2019) and has gained increasing attention among entrepreneurship scholars (McKnight & Zietsma, 2018; Younger & Fisher, 2020). International business (IB) scholars, however, have been notably absent from this contemporary conversation. Very few IB-related studies were covered in the previous reviews of the optimal distinctiveness literature (Zhao et al., 2017; Zhao & Glynn, 2022; Zuckerman, 2016). This is surprising given that the common challenge underpinning optimal distinctiveness – the competing pressures of conformity and differentiation – features prominently in various core IB topics. For example, one key challenge that multinational enterprises (MNEs) face is the dual imperatives of global conformity and local adaptation (Bartlett & Ghoshal, 1989; Kostova & Zaheer, 1999; Pant & Ramachandran, 2017). Competing pressures to simultaneously conform to and differentiate from peers also prevail in the internationalization process as firms make location choices (Delios, Gaur & Makino, 2008), choose entry modes (Oehme & Bort, 2015), and develop firm strategies (Salomon & Wu, 2012).

The lack of attention to optimal distinctiveness among IB scholars indicated in Zhao and colleagues' reviews might be due to their particular review methods. In both reviews (Zhao et al., 2017; Zhao & Glynn, 2022), the authors focused on the five major management journals (*Academy of Management Journal, Academy of Management Review, Administrative Science Quarterly, Organization Science,* and *Strategic Management Journal*) without screening IB-related journals (e.g., *Journal of International Business Studies, Journal of World Business, Global Strategy Journal*). Partly due to this review method, they found that most optimal distinctiveness research to date has focused on organizations in the United States, with only a small number of studies examining organizations in Chinese, Australian, European, and South and Southeast Asian settings.

I see a great opportunity to systematically identify and review optimal distinctiveness-related studies in the IB literature, and, based on this review, to bridge and integrate optimal distinctiveness scholarship in IB, strategy, and organization theory. Such an effort will help depict a more accurate picture of how IB scholars have engaged the optimal distinctiveness notion in their research. It will also allow scholars to compare and cross-tabulate the key insights from this IB-targeted review with major themes from optimal distinctiveness research in strategy and organization theory (as discussed in Section 3). In doing so, scholars can pinpoint IB topics for which optimal distinctiveness is a central concern and identify IB topics that could benefit from engaging more closely with optimal distinctiveness research in other disciplines. Moreover, this IB-targeted review will help uncover important insights; broaden traditional optimal distinctiveness research to international contexts; and open up exciting research opportunities at the interface of optimal distinctiveness and IB scholarship, which remains untapped yet fertile terrain.

Indeed, Zhao and Glynn (2022) alluded to the value of such integration between optimal distinctiveness and IB research by suggesting that optimal distinctiveness research could benefit from attending to the cultural embeddedness of optimal distinctiveness and the cultural shaping of optimal distinctiveness dynamics. In particular, they suggested that broader cultural and societal forces may affect organizations' likelihood and pace of transition from conformity to differentiation. Zhao and Glynn (2022) encouraged scholars to draw insights from cultural psychology to understand how cultural differences in individuals' self-construals lie along the independent-interdependent dimension, which the authors argued bears a strong similarity to the differentiation-conformity dimension of optimal distinctiveness research. The argument is that in some countries (e.g., European-American contexts), societal cultures place a stronger emphasis on individuation of the self and treat the self as a bundle of distinct, positive, and largely idiosyncratic attributes (Markus & Kitayama, 1991). In contrast, in other countries (e.g., Japan and South Korea), societal cultures emphasize interdependence and connectedness (Markus & Kitayama, 1991). These cultural differences led the authors to speculate that the notion of optimal distinctiveness may mean different things and have different implications in Japanese and Korean firms compared to in US and European firms. The former countries may place stronger emphasis on the conformity dimension, whereas the last countries likely place more emphasis on the differentiation dimension. Furthermore, one could imagine that these cultural differences may also shape the temporal dynamics of optimal distinctiveness in that firms operating in countries with a stronger emphasis on interdependence and cooperation may delay their transition from conformity to differentiation. These are all important questions worth further investigation by both optimal distinctiveness and IB scholars.

Furthermore, firms operating in a global context confront multiple institutional pressures from different stakeholders, including stakeholders from their home countries, those in host countries, and other global stakeholders. The question of how to simultaneously balance the need for similarity and differentiation in different contexts and among different stakeholders requires a systematic optimal distinctiveness framework. For instance, within a foreign host country, MNEs need to deal with institutional and market complexity, which manifests as geographic segmentation, sectorial heterogeneity, and fierce competition (Luo, Zhang, & Bu, 2019). Therefore, future research should undertake a systematic analysis to investigate how organizations can use different stakeholders as benchmarks to gauge their optimal distinctiveness as well as how they can achieve optimal distinctiveness through combinations of different organizational dimensions. Moreover, while existing optimal distinctiveness research has focused on institutional theory to explain the legitimacy-seeking rationale for firms' strategic similarity, IB research provides alternative theoretical perspectives to understand other rationales for similarity, including overcoming the liability of foreignness (Wu & Salomon, 2016), enabling spillovers and vicarious learning (Baum, Li, & Usher, 2000), and handling other competitive considerations (Gimeno et al., 2005). Disentangling these alternative rationales behind similarity versus differentiation decisions will further advance research at the intersection of optimal distinctiveness and IB.

Future research will also benefit from adopting a more dynamic view to examine how the optimal balance between similarity and differentiation changes over time. This topic is particularly important for MNEs whose operations coevolve with both global and local institutions. For example, Pant and Ramachandran (2017) explained how Hindustan Unilever sustained a dynamic balance between the dual cores (i.e., enterprise logic and domestic logic) of the subsidiary's espoused identity. Similarly, Tracey and colleagues (2018) showed that the legitimacy pressures entrepreneurs experience vary significantly as ventures mature so that legitimation is an iterative, dynamic, and ongoing accomplishment rather than a "one-off" activity with clear beginning and end points. Still, more IB research is needed to explore how MNEs dynamically maintain optimal distinctiveness as their operations grow into different stages and expand into different institutional contexts.

In sum, IB research provides fertile ground and multiple novel theoretical perspectives to further extend optimal distinctiveness scholarship. Conversely, optimal distinctiveness research offers an intriguing framework to better understand IB questions. A more comprehensive future research agenda at the intersection of IB and optimal distinctiveness awaits.

To recap the key points of this section, I first reiterated some of the core strategic management topics originally proposed by Zhao et al. (2017) that could benefit from incorporating the key insights implied by the orienting conceptual framework. I next discussed how the framework can similarly inform contemporary entrepreneurship and IB research. In doing so, I generated a number of research questions that scholars in these various domains can build on in future studies.

5 Zooming In: How the Optimal Distinctiveness Framework Informs Studies of Organizations' Competitive Positioning

While in Section 4 I discussed how the orienting framework proposed in Section 3 can inform a broad set of topics in various disciplines, in this section, I aim to concretize the value of this framework by focusing on one particular topic – the competitive positioning of organizations. Most theories on the competitive positioning of organizations follow a structural perspective and rest on the assumption that "competition derives from occupying similar positions in resource space" (Ingram & Yue, 2008: 276). In spite of sharing this common assumption, strategic management and organization theory scholars have approached structural similarity in varying ways. Early conceptualizations of competition among strategy scholars were influenced by industrial economics and focused on industry as the locus of competition among similar firms (Porter, 1980). Scholars argued that firms operating in industries characterized by strong competitive forces (e.g., threat of entrants, bargaining power of suppliers, bargaining power of consumers, substitutes, and rivalry) face unfavorable industry environments and will thus find it hard to achieve superior performance (Porter, 1980). In this case, all firms operating in the same industry are considered competitors, so firms are encouraged to pursue differentiation from industry peers in order to stand out and gain competitive advantage (Porter, 1996). Ecological models of competition followed a similar approach in defining all members within the same organizational population as competitors (Hannan & Freeman, 1977; Simons & Ingram, 2004).

Categorizing all firms operating in the same industry/population as equal competitors is an obvious simplification as certain firms compete more intensely with one another than with others. Subsequent research challenged this coarse classification of competitors based on broad industry/population membership and focused on subindustry/subpopulation levels to identify competitors. In fact, even some early conceptualizations strongly rooted in industrial economics and population ecology acknowledged that certain firms may compete more intensely with one another than with others in the same industry. For example, Caves and Porter (1977) introduced the notion of "groups" of firms with differing structural characteristics and discussed mobility barriers between them. Studies of strategic groups later gained traction and took a more heterogeneous view of industries, arguing that an industry comprises diverse groups of firms that share similar strategies (McGee & Thomas, 1986; Peteraf & Shanley, 1997). The notion of strategic groups thus provides an intermediate level of analysis and considers heterogeneity in competitive intensity for different groups within the same industry. Research on strategic groups later lost momentum due to conceptual and empirical challenges in identifying strategic groups and the indecisive findings regarding the performance and competitive implications of strategic group membership (Cattani, Porac, & Thomas, 2017; Dranove, Peteraf, & Shanley, 1998; McGee & Thomas, 1986).

Starting in the 1990s, the resource-based view (RBV) of the firm has become a dominant paradigm and has shifted attention from industry- or strategic group-based conceptualizations of competition to intra-firm resources and capabilities as key determinants of firms' competitive positions (Barney, 1991; Peteraf, 1993; Wernerfelt, 1984). The RBV views firms as bundles of resource and is typically considered as a reaction to earlier conceptualizations of competition based on industry structures or strategic group membership. According to the RBV, a firm's sustainable competitive advantage derives from its ability to develop valuable, rare, and inimitable resources as well as from the organizational structures and coordinating mechanisms it has in place to leverage those resources in an efficient and effective way (Barney, 1991).

Taken together, these theories on competition focus on different levels of analysis (i.e., industry, strategic group, and firm). However, they all take a structural perspective on competition and share a common emphasis on differentiation and uniqueness as a foundational concern in conceptualizing the competitive positioning of firms.

As I have discussed throughout this Element, optimal distinctiveness theory differs from these theories in four key aspects: First, optimal distinctiveness theory puts an equal emphasis on conformity and similarity as foundational considerations in competitive positioning. A certain level of conformity not only ensures firms can cross the legitimacy threshold (McKnight & Zietsma, 2018; Zimmerman & Zeitz, 2002) but can also become a source of distinction itself (Durand & Kremp, 2016). Second, optimal distinctiveness theory attends to the multidimensionality of organizational features and actions and transcends multiple levels of analysis. It encompasses broader environmental conditions, industry and market structures, and organizational resources and attributes in conceptualizing how organizations develop optimally distinct positioning strategies and beat their competition (Barlow et al., 2019; Gupta et al., 2020; Haans, 2019; McKnight & Zietsma, 2018; Zhao et al., 2017). Third, compared to the structural perspectives of competition, optimal distinctiveness theory takes a socio-cognitive perspective and conceptualizes competitive positioning as resulting from a dynamic cognitive process where actors (e.g., managers, entrepreneurs) attend to and interpret market cues from other market participants (e.g., consumers, suppliers, and competitors) and make corresponding strategic choices based on those perceptions and interpretations (Porac et al., 1989). Fourth, according to optimal distinctiveness theory, organizations compete in environments enacted by multiple audiences with heterogeneous expectations. Therefore, industry and market boundaries and the competitive dynamics happening therein are contingent on the specific audience constructing them and the relevant benchmarks that audience uses in gauging optimal distinctiveness.

Grounded in these key insights, I next use four empirical examples to illustrate both the conceptual and analytical implications of the orienting optimal distinctiveness framework for understanding organizations' optimal positioning strategies. First, to address the multidimensionality element of the optimal distinctiveness framework, I discuss McKnight and Zietsma's (2018) study of Canadian-based cleantech firms, in which the authors examined how cleantech firms' configurations of six conditions were related to their optimal distinctiveness, which in turn enabled their successful commercialization. Second, I use the console video game market to demonstrate the temporal dynamics of optimal distinctiveness – that is, how organizations need to adjust their positioning strategies dynamically in order to remain optimally distinct as they receive new market cues from key stakeholders (e.g., consumers, critics) and as new markets evolve. Finally, I use stock analysts' evaluations of US public firms and different frontal design decisions of passenger car models to demonstrate the importance of attending to dual benchmarks in gauging optimal distinctiveness and the intricacy that organizations face in strategic positioning to gain audiences' attention and favorable evaluations in dual benchmark settings.

5.1 The Multidimensionality of Optimal Distinctiveness and the Competitive Positioning of Canadian Cleantech Ventures

Clean technology (cleantech) is emerging at an explosive rate to meet the unprecedented global demand for cleaner and more efficient use of energy and resources. Cleantech includes a broad range of "products, services, and processes that harness renewable materials and energy sources, dramatically reduce the use of natural resources, and cut or eliminate emissions and wastes" (Wikipedia). Because of its promise of supporting a sustainable business approach, investments in cleantech have grown considerably around the world. In spite of this progress, cleantech is still "an emerging industry with few successfully legitimated models" (McKnight & Zietsma, 2018: 495). Therefore, to achieve the goal, cleantech firms need first to transform from being new ventures to successfully commercialized businesses.

McKnight and Zietsma (2018) conducted a study of thirty Canadian-based cleantech ventures located in Ontario and British Columbia and examined the various pathways for those ventures to achieve successful commercialization. In this setting, gaining legitimacy for new ventures and innovations is difficult, but also important for attracting resources from various stakeholders such as capital providers, customers and potential employees. At the same time, standing out from both other new ventures and incumbent firms is also critical for competing for finance and winning customers. As such, optimal distinctiveness is a strong imperative for cleantech ventures' successful commercialization. The first analytical step of this study is then to identify a set of organizational strategies and conditions that are most relevant in shaping both the legitimacy and differentiation of cleantech ventures and in turn their commercialization outcomes.

The authors used both deductive and inductive approaches in identifying these strategies and conditions. Deductively, the authors resorted to prior optimal distinctiveness literature and identified four factors that have been suggested to significantly influence firms' legitimacy and differentiation. Inductively, the authors conducted semi-structured interviews with a senior manager of each firm in the sample and further identified two factors that may affect a firm's commercialization outcome. The six factors involve a variety of firm strategies and conditions and include (1) differentiating framing (a frame that problematizes current approaches and paints new technologies as different from existing technologies), (2) collaborative strategy (whether a cleantech firm works with other cleantech firms by actively participating in cleantech associations, working committees, industry groups, or other alliances), (3) radical technology (whether a firm develops a fundamentally new technology offering a clear departure from existing practices), (4) incumbent dependency (whether incumbent firms strongly control access to either technology platforms or customer bases), (5) prior relevant experience (whether the entrepreneur engaged in past entrepreneurial activity or top management activity in cleantech), and (6) international presence (whether a firm displays evidence of a strong presence in international markets beyond Canada).

The authors then employed QCA to examine how cleantech firms' configurations of the six factors are related to successful commercialization. These six factors lead to a total of sixty-four (2^6) possible configurations of firm attributes. The authors narrowed these sixty-four configurations down to a smaller number of unique configurations based on certain consistency and frequency thresholds. Six equifinal configurations were ultimately identified as being associated with the successful commercialization of Canadian cleantech firms.

This study represents an important empirical advancement in optimal distinctiveness research. Applying QCA enabled the authors to address the multi-dimensionality of optimal distinctiveness head on. Different combinations of firm characteristics, symbolic actions, and strategic practices were found to help cleantech ventures cross the legitimacy threshold and achieve differentiation, which together led to their successful commercialization. This study provides supporting evidence for the ideas that there are multiple pathways through which firms can achieve optimal distinctiveness and that different organizational dimensions can be managed and orchestrated in unique patterns yet contribute to equally optimal performance outcomes.

The authors' employment of both deductive and inductive approaches in identifying the six organizational strategies and conditions also provides a useful approach for addressing the infinite dimensionality problem discussed earlier. Both a good understanding of the literature and deep knowledge of the cases and empirical context help narrow scholars' attention down to a manageable number of most salient and relevant organizational dimensions. This approach is especially useful in small-N settings, i.e., settings with a small number of cases for which scholars can gain access and acquire deep insights on the cases. Deep knowledge on the cases also helps alleviate the concern of scholars overlooking certain underlying organizational strategies and conditions that drive the outcome, yet are difficult to observe and measure – what we call *omitted causal conditions*. However, in large-N settings, the issue of omitted causal conditions may loom large. Scholars using QCA in large-N settings need to be conscious of this potential problem and closely follow methodological advances that may help address this issue.

5.2 The Temporal Dynamics of Optimal Distinctiveness and the Competitive Positioning of Video Games in Evolving Markets

5.2.1 Emerging and Evolving Market Spaces in the Console Video Game Industry

The console video game market, like other cultural industries, is characterized by high uncertainty and constantly shifting preferences in consumer (i.e., gamer) tastes (Loguidice & Barton, 2009). New types of game and generations of platforms are created in an effort to chase and corral tastes. As part of this process, game publishers and their developers attempt to sense gamers' preferences and hope that the products they launch will become hits. Before a game's release, in order to influence gamers' perceptions and increase the chance of market success, publishers often engage in elaborate media campaigns. On a game's launch, there is an inevitable buzz among gamers about the merits (and demerits) of the product experience, which is generated via public and private online opinion forums. Well-recognized game critics also assess games, partly providing forums for the buzz, but also offering their own independent reviews and delineating the pros and cons of new games.

Despite all these prelaunch efforts, gamers' tastes and each product's success remain largely unpredictable in advance. Only a limited number of original games, known as "hit games," are launched with great success. These big hits normally become recognized quickly due to their prominent market success immediately after release and their widely acclaimed technical and aesthetic merits in the media. One key component of these success stories revolves around the novel creation or (re)combination of game features (Arsenault, 2009). In the case of *Elder Scrolls IV: Oblivion*, for example, game critics highly praised its novel combination of action, role-playing, and fantasy in one game. Indeed, Eurogamer editor Kristan Reed (2006) stated that *Oblivion* "successfully unites some of the best elements of RPG [role-playing game], adventure and action games and fuses them into a relentlessly immersive and intoxicating whole." Gamers also valued this novel combination of game features, with one gamer saying that "you will play for hours ... say goodbye to the girl" (Dayin, 2007). Partly because of their novel combination of game features and the critical acclaim around it, games like *Oblivion* tend to achieve high sales right after release, immediately and strongly signaling to potential entrants that they are the most salient exemplars around which new game categories are being recognized and promoted by industry media and participants.

The creation of a big hit with novel combinations of game features – an exemplar – is a key moment in the emergence of a new video game category. More importantly, exemplary hit games immediately begin to influence other publishers' game designs and development. For instance, the success of *Grand Theft Auto III* has stimulated a series of "GTA clones" (e.g., *Mafia, The Getaway, True Crime*, etc.). All these games combine action, racing/driving, and shooter features and immerse gamers in story-driven, open-ended urban environments that incorporate driving and attacking capabilities as well as violence and crime themes. In fact, the development of new games around exemplary hit games is an essential part of the emergence of a new game category. For instance, the CEO of one video game publisher put it this way:

> When a hit game is released, a new formula is found. It is further developed and perfected by the continued development of similar games. New game genres typically emerge out of these new formulas which have been taken further by clones. Cloning is often how entire genres are born!

A senior product manager of another video game publisher similarly commented, "Entire game genres typically have emerged by mimicking and extending on great games."

However, not all games entering a new category are created equal. While some games are effortless endeavors that enter an emerging category simply to cash in on the new trend, others end up being innovative, and some even surpass the original inspiration. Industry experts have emphasized this point, arguing that some new entrants have "indeed [been] little more than derivative products with a new skin but the same game underneath, [but] many [have] at least tried a few things. In these cases, the game creators went for revision instead of replication" (Arsenault, 2009: 166). Therefore, new entrants' strategic positioning against exemplary hit games seems to vary, leading to vastly different performance outcomes.

5.2.2 Optimal Positioning Strategies in Evolving Markets

In a more recent study, Zhao et al. (2018) focused on examining how new entrants' different positioning strategies vis-à-vis exemplary hit games affected these entrants' performance. Empirically, the authors studied new video game categories that emerged and evolved around exemplary hit games. Given that most of these new video game categories were new groupings of games that were only weakly entrenched and their potential to become widely institutionalized remained to be seen, the authors called these new market categories "proto-categories." Indeed, some of proto-categories become increasingly populated and thus become institutionalized over time, whereas others fizzle and can best be considered a kind of fad or fashion (Abrahamson, 1991). Regardless of their ultimate fate, such proto-categories can shape the attention and behavior of producers and consumers in a product market, and thus influence the competitive dynamics. In the paper, Zhao et al. (2018) sought to address the following research questions: How does the strategic differentiation of a new product offering vis-à-vis the exemplar of a proto-category affect the offering's market performance? How does the performance impact of strategic differentiation change as a proto-category evolves? What are the underlying mechanisms driving the observed effects?

To answer these questions, the authors first had to identify exemplar hit games and the proto-categories that emerged and formed around those hits. To do so, they first compiled all console video games launched in the US market between 1995 and 2012. After game compilations, expansion packs, and add-ons were excluded, the initial sample for analysis consisted of 9,024 standalone games. Important game demographic information (e.g., publishers, developers, release details, features, and critics' ratings) and sales data were collected from two widely used databases for video game research: MobyGames and NPD. The authors then set out to identify exemplary hit games out of the 9,024 games in the initial sample. Given that exemplars are defined as games that enjoyed great critical acclaim and market success, they used two key criteria in identifying them. First, they narrowed the initial sample to those games whose sales are one standard deviation above the average total sales of the 9,024 games. This step ensured the selection of industry top performers that best qualified as exemplars for others. Second, the authors selected games that appeared on at least one of the five "greatest games" charts created by five notable game magazines/websites: Electronic Game Monthly (top 200 games), IGN (top 100 games), G4TV (top 100 games), GameRankings (top 100 games), and Gamer Informer (top 100 games). This second criterion ensured that games identified were widely broadcasted as successful and innovative in popular product reviews and industry magazines. Applying the two criteria yielded 163 potential exemplars around which proto-categories formed or were forming. Further affirming their exemplar status, most of the 163 games gained substantial market reception and garnered important awards soon after their formal release.

With the 163 exemplars identified, the next task was to pinpoint the game features of the exemplars that appealed to potential market entrants. To do so, the authors collected extensive text data on each of the exemplars, including detailed game descriptions, award information, and critic reviews. These text data were useful since they contained important information regarding standard game dimensions (e.g., gameplay, sound, and graphics) and storyline as well as discussions of the games' premium new features. The authors scrutinized the text data to discern the "core" features that defined and distinguished each exemplar. These core features and their combinations were viewed by game critics and users as new, refined, and/or superior to those in other games at the time. By following this coding process, the authors further narrowed the 163 games to seventy-eight exemplars since these seventy-eight games had unique core features, were widely regarded as the greatest games of their time, attracted substantial gamer interest, and significantly influenced and inspired subsequent game design. The remaining eighty-five games shared core features with the seventy-right exemplars mainly because the eighty-five games were released as sequels and were thus considered as important renewals of the proto-categories that formed around the seventy-eight exemplary hit games.

The core features of each of the seventy-eight exemplars set a provisional boundary for each corresponding proto-category and helped discriminate between members and nonmembers of these categories. New entrants to these proto-categories were then defined as those games that were released after the exemplary hit games and shared the same core features with the exemplars. Note that despite the common core features shared between the new entrants and the corresponding exemplars, their other features can vary. In other words, the common core does not preclude variations among entrants within the same proto-category. Indeed, legitimate members of a category may not be uniform; they may vary in their degree of membership and may be considered as members of numerous different proto-categories (Hannan, Pólos, & Carroll, 2007; Rao, Morrill, & Zald, 2000). This coding procedure resulted in a total of 6,544 unique entrants in the seventy-eight proto-categories.

Figure 3 illustrates the seventy-eight proto-categories and all their entrants using a multidimensional scaling plot based on the Euclidean distances between the core features of each pair of the seventy-eight proto-categories in 1996, 2001, 2006, and 2011. Each of the seventy-eight proto-categories is indicated by a solid bubble. The color of each bubble reflects its order of release, with darker colors indicating exemplars released earlier. The size of each bubble reflects the cumulative number of entrants in the proto-category, with larger sizes indicating proto-categories with more entrants. As shown in the figure, the distances between the seventy-eight proto-categories vary as does their popularity in terms of number of entrants. Older proto-categories have normally (but not necessarily) attracted more entrants over time.

The primary focus in this project was to examine the impact of strategic differentiation between an entrant game and the exemplar on the entrant's performance and how this impact changes as the proto-category evolves. The authors' central proposition is that in the early stage of a proto-category's evolution, it is optimal for new entrants to conform to the exemplar's features, because at this stage, the exemplar serves as a strong and salient reference point for new entrants. The exemplar is also considered an important benchmark and yardstick against which game critics evaluate the new entrants. Therefore, critics' ratings and consumers' choices are strongly framed by the exemplar and its unique feature combinations, which means that conformity pressures are particularly strong at this stage. At the same time, competitive pressures and the

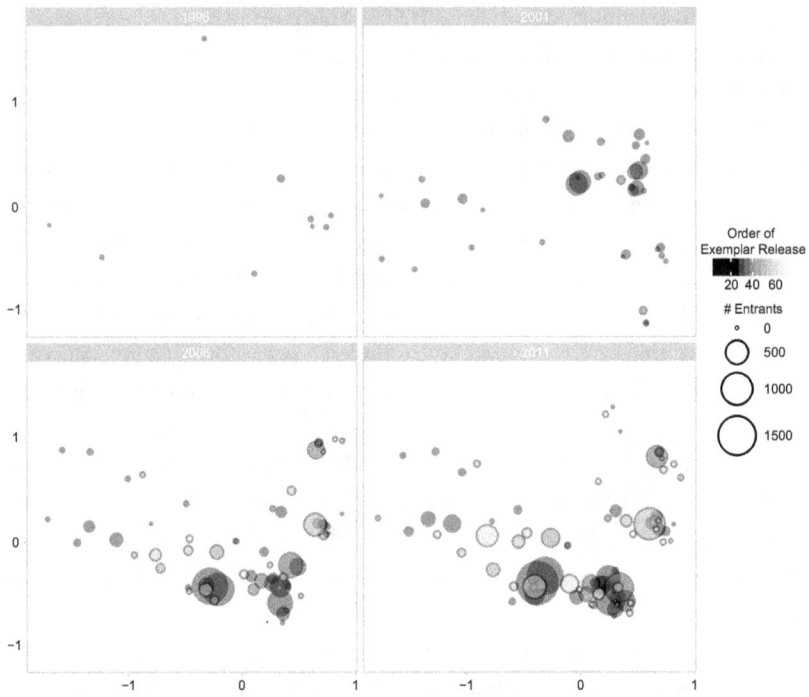

Figure 3 Multidimensional scaling (MDS) plot of the proto-categories at four
time points
Reprinted with permission from Zhao et al. (2018)

imperatives for differentiation are relatively weak given the nascency of the
market space, which is characterized by a limited number of other entrants.

As the proto-category evolves, the relative strengths of conformity and differentiation pressures change. Specifically, the market space becomes increasingly more
crowded with new entrants, escalating competitive pressures among all games in
the market. Both critics and consumers may also become progressively satiated
with old games and thus demand for new features. All these forces together may
push new entrants to differentiate themselves in a more crowded market space
(Navis & Glynn, 2010; Wry et al., 2011). At this stage, conformity pressures may
remain strong. While differentiation from the exemplar is increasingly appreciated,
extreme deviations from the exemplar still risks being screened out of consideration and losing appeal to key audiences (Zuckerman, 1999). Therefore, as the
proto-category evolves, an intermediate positioning strategy vis-à-vis the exemplar
may become optimal for enhancing entrants' performance. Overall, then,
a temporal dynamic in optimal distinctiveness is expected in the video game
industry: in the early stage of proto-category emergence, conformity to the

exemplar's features helps enhance entrants' performance; as the proto-category evolves, there is increasing demand for differentiation, so an intermediately differentiated positioning strategy against the exemplar's features is optimal for enhancing entrants' performance.

In addition, the authors highlighted the role of game critics in mediating the impact of strategic differentiation on entrants' performance and expected that this mediating effect is increasingly salient as a proto-category evolves for two reasons. First, in a more crowded market space, there is increasing evaluative complexity, so it is more difficult for consumers to sort through the growing thicket of competing games and their features. In this case, critics' mediating role becomes more important. Second, at later stages of proto-category evolution, critics – as compared to typical consumers – are more likely to act as "market makers" who embrace innovations and endorse stronger differentiation (Pontikes, 2012).

Analyzing the 6,544 games that entered the seventy-eight proto-categories, the authors found strong support for these predictions. The key findings are plotted in Figure 4, which vividly illustrates the temporal dynamics of optimal distinctiveness (the curve flips from a U-shape to an inverted U-shape as the market evolves). This project is among the first to conceptualize and empirically test the dynamic nature of optimal distinctiveness. Studying a dynamic entrepreneurial environment characterized by demand uncertainty allowed the authors to theorize on the underlying mechanisms – namely, the varying strengths of conformity versus differentiation pressures – and foreground the mediating role of important intermediaries (e.g., critics), both of which have received limited attention in previous optimal distinctiveness research. Future research should attend to such temporal dynamics in optimal competitive positioning and continue to unpack the underlying mechanisms that drive the temporal shift from conformity to differentiation (or vice versa).

5.3 Competitive Positioning in Dual Benchmark Settings

As I discussed in Section 3, identifying and theorizing on the benchmarks for gauging optimal distinctiveness constitutes an important element of the orienting conceptual framework. Most studies of optimal distinctiveness to date have either explicitly or implicitly assumed that an organization's optimal distinctiveness is gauged against a single benchmark. Following this approach, past studies have identified benchmarks that are either externally derived based on category prototypes, exemplars, or substitutes (e.g., McDonald & Eisenhardt, 2020; Zhao et al., 2018) or internally driven by founder identity or aspirations

(a) Use time since exemplar release to track proto-category evolution

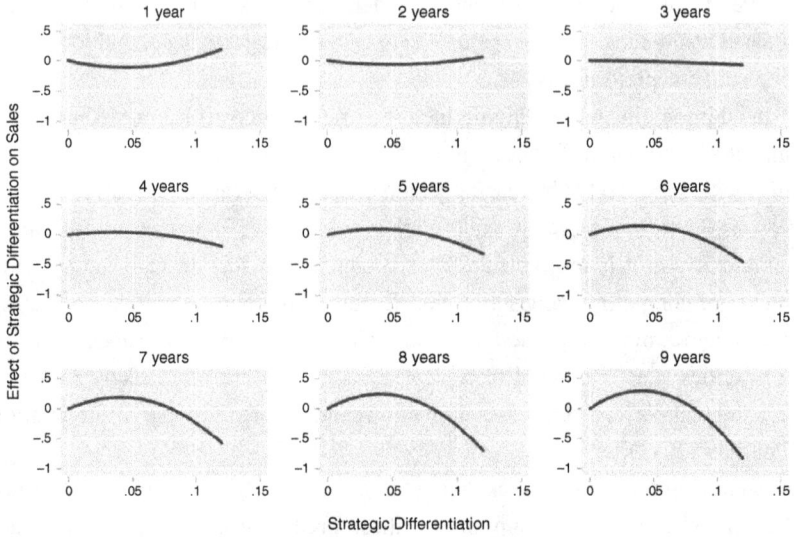

(b) Use number of prior entrants to track proto-category evolution

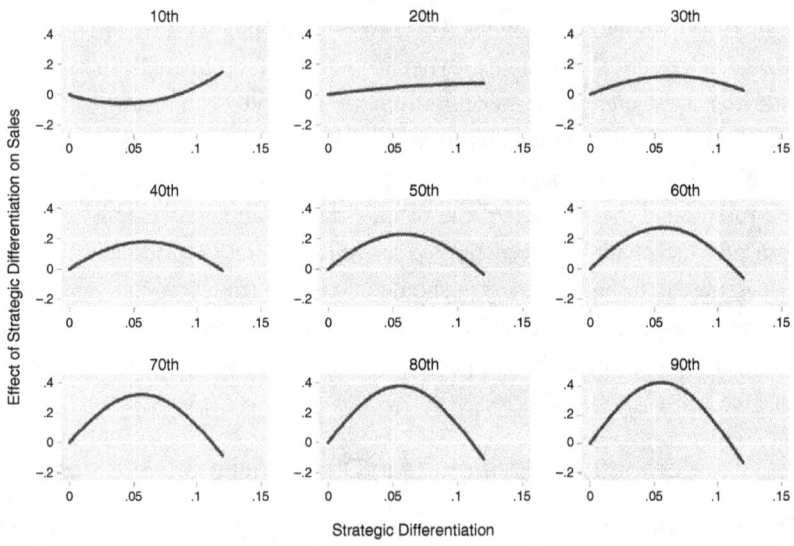

Figure 4 The temporal effect of strategic differentiation on game sales
Reprinted with permission from Zhao et al. (2018)

(e.g., Grimes, 2018; Zuzul & Tripsas, 2020). The focus of this work has mainly been examining how conforming to or differentiating from one particular type of benchmark shapes organizational actions and performance outcomes. This approach of focusing on one benchmark is conceptually parsimonious and empirically tractable. However, it is far from reflecting reality and falls short in explaining scenarios in which two or more relevant and distinct benchmarks coexist – scenarios I call dual benchmark settings.

Attending to dual benchmark settings is important because stakeholders in such settings may resort to divergent reference points in perceiving and evaluating organizations, and organizations in turn are faced with more challenges and complexities in understanding these different benchmarks and formulating their optimal positioning strategies accordingly. Practically, dual benchmark settings are also prevalent, and in many industries exemplars may diverge from the prototype (e.g., Tesla is an exemplar in the automobile industry that deviates from a prototypical automaker). While most past research on optimal distinctiveness has examined the performance implications of firms' similarities to either the prototype or an exemplar, scenarios in which there are dual or many coexisting, relevant, and distinct benchmarks present the most complex yet interesting cases for both researchers and practitioners (Barlow et al., 2019; Tracey et al., 2018). Zhao and Glynn (2022: 19–20) alluded to this challenge and raised a number of research questions for scholars to address in future research:

> How do audiences pick which benchmark to use in attending to and evaluating an organization? Is there a sequence in terms of how audiences apply these alternative benchmarks? If so, in what order and what determines the order? In light of these alternative benchmarks, how would organizations position themselves in order to be optimally distinct? Will an organization's conformity (versus differentiation) against one benchmark impact audience perceptions and evaluations or will this impact vary depending on its conformity (versus differentiation) against another benchmark? Addressing such dual or multiple benchmark challenges will generate important insights regarding the complexity of organizations' strategic moves and the corresponding audience responses.

Further complicating the issue is the possibility that different benchmarks may either exist at the same level or exist at different levels of analysis; this latter possibility requires and provides an opportunity for us to conceptualize and analyze optimal distinctiveness as a multilevel construct. In this section, I draw on two empirical settings in which dual benchmarks exist to discuss how scholars can approach the above-mentioned research questions: the first regards financial analysts' evaluations of US public firms against both industry exemplars and industry prototypes; and the second regards automakers' design of car models against both industry- and organizational-level prototypical designs.

5.3.1 Financial Analysts and Their Evaluations of US Public Firms

Contrary to the efficient-market hypothesis, which assumes minimal uncertainty in stock evaluations (Fama, 1965; Miller & Modigliani, 1961), the sociological view of stock markets argues that investors face strong valuation challenges due to "the inherent unpredictability of the economic future" and their cognitive limits in processing information (Zuckerman, 1999: 1411). In markets where investors face significant valuation challenges, financial analysts serve as surrogate investors and are considered "visible and knowledgeable experts who constantly collect, analyze, and disseminate information about the future prospects of publicly listed firms" (Brauer & Wiersema, 2018: 218). As such, financial analysts play an important intermediary role, functioning as information brokers and monitors on behalf of investors and providing recommendations and endorsements on public firms' prospects (Jensen, 2004; Litov, Moreton, & Zenger, 2012). Consequently, public firms' market values are affected by financial analysts' coverage and recommendations (Litov, Moreton, & Zenger, 2012; Zuckerman, 1999).

Financial analysts pursue industry-based division of labor and typically track the performance of firms from the same industry (Zuckerman, 1999). Acting as critics of firms' stocks in a particular industry, financial analysts' coverage and recommendations of stocks have both been suggested to influence firms' market values. Financial analysts' coverage of a firm attests to the firm's legitimacy as a member of its market category (Jensen, 2004; Zuckerman, 1999). When a firm receives more coverage from financial analysts who specialize in its industry, it indicates that the firm has been successful in signaling and establishing its identity. In contrast, failure to garner industry-specialized analyst coverage signals a mismatch between a firm's self-definition and the financial analysts' perceptions of its market positioning, leading to confusion over the firm's identity and consequently a reduced stock price (Zuckerman, 1999). After making their coverage decisions, financial analysts evaluate the selected stocks to decide whether they are under- or overvalued and accordingly offer advices for investors to buy, sell, or hold their shares (Feldman, 2016; Westphal & Clement, 2008). For example, the Institutional Brokers' Estimate System gathers and compiles financial analysts' estimates on the future earnings of the majority of US publicly traded companies and standardizes analysts' recommendation scales to five categories: strong buy, buy, hold, sell, and strong sell.

However, these five-category recommendation scales are deceptively simple and conceal the complex valuation processes and varied valuation approaches used by individual financial analysts. Among the various valuation approaches, the relative valuation approach is of paramount relevance in financial analysts' valuation practices (Meitner, 2006). Compared to the direct valuation approach, which is based on the net present values of stocks calculated using the discounted cash flow method, the relative valuation method is "based on the principle of arbitrage and values companies based on how other, similar companies are valued" (Meitner, 2006: 1). While the relative valuation method has been criticized for its lack of theoretical foundation and has been labeled a "quick and dirty method of valuation" (Benninga & Sarig, 1997: 330), it has gained wide recognition and popularity among practitioners because it is straightforward for financial analysts to apply and easier to present to investors than direct valuations (Meitner, 2006).

In applying the relative valuation approach, financial analysts' first core task is to identify comparable companies that share certain characteristics with the target company under evaluation. There are different ways of determining what specific characteristics comparable companies and the target company need to have in common. The ideal case is to find firms that are similar on a number of important firm attributes, such as products or services offered, distribution channels and types of customers, competition level of the industry, etc. However, with an increasing number of firm characteristics considered, the difficulty of finding comparable firms that match on all attributes is compounded. In fact, possible comparable firms are quickly exhausted given the limited number of public firms and the fact that no two companies are completely identical.

To overcome these challenges in identifying and selecting comparable firms, financial analysts normally resort to the industry criterion assuming that companies in the same industry share a lot in common (e.g., the nature and degree of competition). Furthermore, they tend to gauge a target firm against two benchmarks within an industry boundary and evaluate the firm based on its similarity to the benchmarks. The default benchmark financial analysts normally use is the industry prototype, which is captured by the mean attributes of all firms in the same industry as the target firm (Meitner, 2006). Firms that have attributes that are close to the industry prototype are considered more typical firms. Another benchmark financial analysts may use to gauge a target firm is exemplary firms in the same industry. Exemplary firms are outstanding, high-performing firms in the industry, which have been shown to be important reference points for comparisons and evaluations of peer firms in the same industry (Nosofsky & Johansen, 2000; Smith & Zarate, 1992; Zhao et al., 2018).

Given these two distinct benchmarks, the important question for both scholars and practitioners is then how US public firms' similarity to industry prototypes and similarity to exemplars jointly shape financial analysts' attention to and evaluations of these firms, and, consequently, firms' market values. Majzoubi and colleagues (2021) recently conducted a large-scale study of US public firms to address this question. Building on developments in the optimal distinctiveness literature that recognize industry exemplars as important benchmarks for firms' positioning and audience evaluations (e.g., Barlow et al., 2019; Zhao et al., 2018), the authors theorize how firms' similarity to industry exemplars, which they call exemplar similarity, affects financial analysts' coverage (through the mechanism of association) and recommendations (through the mechanism of comparison), which in turn influence the firms' market values (an outcome jointly shaped by the association and comparison mechanisms). Furthermore, the authors argue that the impact of exemplar similarity on a firm's market value varies depending on the firm's typicality – the degree to which the firm is similar to the industry prototype. This is because the strengths of the two mechanisms – association and comparison – differ for typical firms (versus atypical firms) that already enjoy a certain degree of legitimacy and recognizability and are more likely to be compared with industry prototypes as default benchmarks.

Majzoubi and colleagues' (2021) study generated three key findings. First, firms can garner analysts' attention and legitimacy by positioning near a well-known exemplar firm. Therefore, higher exemplar similarity contributes to association benefit and in turn leads to higher analyst coverage. Second, higher exemplar similarity also places a firm and an exemplar side by side, thereby increasing the firm's chance of being compared with the exemplar and receiving discounted analyst evaluations in the form of lower investment recommendations. The contrasting effects of exemplar similarity on analysts' coverage and recommendations prompted the authors to examine its overall impact on firms' market values. The third and perhaps most intriguing finding is that the impact of exemplar similarity on a firm's market value varies depending on the degree of the firm's typicality. A typical firm should choose a moderately differentiated positioning strategy to maximize its market value, whereas an atypical firm should pursue either a highly conforming or highly differentiating positioning strategy.

These findings advance optimal distinctiveness research by confirming the idea of the dual benchmark challenge and elaborating on the implications of this challenge for firms' positioning strategies and associated performance outcomes. In particular, the authors addressed the dual benchmark challenge head on and revealed some intricate relationships between firms' positioning strategies and performance outcomes when industry prototypes and exemplars both serve as important reference points in audience evaluations. The theory and findings of this project also enrich our understanding of the underlying mechanisms that drive optimal positioning strategies. As discussed in earlier sections of this Element, most previous studies in the literature have focused on theorizing two competing mechanisms – legitimacy and competition – and have argued that what constitutes an optimally positioning strategy depends on the nature and relative strengths of these two mechanisms (e.g., Deephouse, 1999; Haans, 2019; Zhao et al., 2018). This study goes beyond these two mechanisms and highlights association benefit and comparison cost as two important yet underexplored mechanisms in optimal distinctiveness research. Furthermore, as a firm moves closer to an exemplar (i.e., as exemplar similarity increases), the salience and relative strength of association benefit and comparison cost do not change in a uniform pattern but depend on the degree of the firm's typicality. As such, audience evaluations of a firm's conformity to (or differentiation from) one benchmark (e.g., an exemplar) hinges on the firm's conformity to (or differentiation from) another benchmark (e.g., the prototype).

Moreover, Zhao et al. (2017) criticized the lack of attention given to stakeholder perceptions and evaluations in previous studies of the positioning-performance relationship. Recent studies have started to respond to this criticism by bringing the mediating role of stakeholders to the fore and theorizing on how different positioning strategies affect stakeholder evaluations (e.g., Zhao et al., 2018). This study further extends this line of inquiry by disentangling the effects of firms' positioning on stakeholder attention and stakeholder evaluations (in this case, the stakeholders are financial analysts). The authors conceptually and empirically confirmed the idea that exemplar similarity can have contrasting effects on these two important audience-related outcomes even though both contribute to positive firm market values. The contrasting effects then creates a dilemma for firms as they decide how close they want to position themselves to industry exemplars. This dilemma can only be resolved after the dual benchmark challenge is acknowledged and firms' typicality is taken into account.

5.3.2 Automakers' Design of Car Models Against Industry- and Organizational-Level Benchmarks

Another dual benchmark setting that has received limited attention in optimal distinctiveness research is multiproduct organizations. Most studies on optimal distinctiveness have focused on the organizational level and examined how organizations can optimally position against peers. However, the same tension between conformity and differentiation can manifest not only between organizations but also within organizations (particularly within multiproduct organizations). Indeed, the need to balance the competing demands for differentiation and conformity both within and between organizations "has become increasingly imperative as many organizations expand their product lines and develop a variety of products to increase competitiveness and consumer loyalty" (Bu et al., 2022: 2). Therefore, understanding how organizations can simultaneously balance the tensions between differentiation and conformity in inter- and intra-organizational contexts is both theoretically and practically important. In the context of multiproduct organizations, various questions arise: "First, to what extent should their products be distinct from those of other organizations? Second, to what extent should their products be distinct from other products within their own organization? Third, how can organizations effectively orchestrate the distinctiveness at multiple levels?" (Bu et al., 2022: 2–3).

To answer these questions, scholars need to develop a multilevel framework to study optimal distinctiveness at two different levels. Bu and colleagues (2022) recently took on this endeavor by conceptualizing optimal distinctiveness as a multilevel construct and defining and examining within-organization distinctiveness and between-organization distinctiveness. The former refers to product-level distinctiveness that captures the degree to which a product deviates from the product prototype of its organization, whereas the latter refers to organization-level distinctiveness that captures the degree to which an organization's product prototype deviates from that of the entire industry. Bu et al. (2022) argued that distinctiveness conceptualized at the two different levels have different performance implications. This is because distinctiveness can be evaluated differently at these two different levels since gauging distinctiveness at the two levels entails different benchmarks for comparison and evokes different frames of reference, which results in varied importance of conformity and differentiation pressures.

The authors tested these ideas by analyzing 2,203 model-year observations of automobiles sold in the US market from 2001 to 2016. In particular, they focused on the distinctiveness of frontal design of car models because the frontal design has been increasingly recognized as one of the most important factors shaping consumers' purchasing decisions and thus considered one of the most important drivers of automakers' market performance. Grounded in this context, the authors measured within-organization distinctiveness of a car model's design as the extent to which the focal car model's design is distinct from the prototypical design of all car models produced by the same automaker, and between-organization distinctiveness as the extent to which a focal automaker's prototypical product design is distinct from the prototypical design of the industry. The authors then employed multilevel modeling to estimate how within-organization distinctiveness and between-organization distinctiveness independently and jointly shape a car model's market sales.

Three key findings emerged from this study. First, within-organization distinctiveness of car design hampers car model's sales because categorization is more important than competition in a within-organization context. In this case, consumers tend to have strong brand-specific expectations and thus expect the design of a car model to conform to its organization's prototypical design. For example, a BMW model with no twin-kidney grille in its frontal design would be hardly recognized as a member of the BMW family. At the same time, the differentiation pressure is alleviated because organizations can differentiate their products not only on design but through other dimensions such as size, function, and feature. Differentiation on these other features is frequently used to avoid cannibalization among an organization's own products. Overall, the conformity pressure dominates the differentiation pressure in terms of product design in the intra-organizational context, leading to a negative impact of within-organization distinctiveness of product design on market performance.

Second, in the between-organization context, consumers compare the design of an automaker's prototypical design with the average design in the industry. Since categorization at the industry level (e.g., recognizing an automaker's product as a product of the automotive industry) is based on a product's general shapes and basic functions, consumers' expectations of the average design in the industry tend to be abstract and not as specific as their expectations of the design of a particular brand. Therefore, categorization at the industry level is relatively simple and the conformity pressure is reduced. At the same time, product design is an important differentiator for organizations to win competition at the industry level because organizations increasingly converge on functions and technologies of their products. Overall, then, the differentiation pressure outweighs the conformity pressure in the inter-organizational context, and thus between-organization distinctiveness of product design enhances market performance.

Third, the impacts of within- and between-organization distinctiveness of product design on performance are not independent but interactive. Specifically, the negative impact of within-organization distinctiveness on performance is attenuated when between-organization distinctiveness is high. This is because high between-organization distinctiveness of product design contributes to an identity of "being unconventional". In this case, high within-organization distinctiveness of product design is consistent with this unconventional identity and thus causes less loss of legitimacy.

These findings have important implications for optimal distinctiveness research. The conceptualization of optimal distinctiveness as a multilevel construct directs scholars' attention to different benchmarks consumers may use to perceive and evaluate a product's distinctiveness in within- and between-organization contexts. This represents a significant theoretical advancement because most studies to date on optimal distinctiveness have focused on the between-organization level and assumed that consumers evaluate an organization and its product/service against either industry prototypes or industry exemplars. To the extent that past studies have studied dual benchmark settings and examined how differentiation from prototypes and exemplars jointly shape market performance, the focus is still on different benchmarks at the same level of analysis. However, in multiproduct organizations, consumers' benchmarks for evaluation may shift across different levels, e.g., from the industry-level prototype to the organization-level prototype. By extending the notion of benchmarks under a multilevel framework, Bu et al. (2022) suggest that organizations can strategize the degrees of conformity and differentiation in one organizational dimension (e.g., a car's frontal design) both across their different products and across organizations in the same industry. Therefore, organizations need not only to identify and orchestrate different organizational dimensions to address the conformity-differentiation tension, but also need to carefully manage their distinctiveness at different levels to achieve optimal distinctiveness.

The notion of optimal distinctiveness as a multilevel construct that entails multiple benchmarks also generalizes beyond the context of multiproduct organizations. Recall that in Section 4.2, I discussed the implications of the orienting conceptual framework for entrepreneurship research. One additional research opportunity here is to more seriously consider how optimal distinctiveness transcends multiple levels of analysis in entrepreneurial settings. For example, many startups are essentially one-person operations or are at least strongly influenced by founders' own identities and aspirations. In this case, the original individual-level quest for assimilation and differentiation may be intertwined with firm-level strategic considerations for being optimally distinct. Such settings provide a unique platform for scholars to revisit the social psychological foundations of optimal distinctiveness research and build a bridge between the micro and macro perspectives of optimal distinctiveness scholarship.

To quickly sum up, in this section, I zoomed in on one specific research topic – the competitive positioning of organizations – and demonstrated how the orienting optimal distinctiveness framework can inform and guide empirical research addressing this topic beyond traditional strategy and organization theories on competition. The four empirical studies I featured in this section only scratched the surface of this subject and more opportunities awaits to be explored by scholars interested in studying competitive positioning of organizations.

6 Zooming Out: How the Optimal Distinctiveness Framework Informs Studies of Market Category Dynamics

Section 5.3.2 showcased how optimal distinctiveness can be conceptualized at both within- and between-organization levels. In this section, I zoom out and highlight how the orienting framework can also inform studies of optimal distinctiveness at higher levels of analysis. In particular, I examine how the emergence and evolution of market categories can essentially be conceptualized as an ongoing process in pursuit of optimal distinctiveness. I use the emergence and development of H-Farm, a form of business incubator in Italy, as an empirical example to illustrate the idea.

Market categories play fundamental roles in establishing meaning systems, setting audiences' expectations, and structuring and governing market transactions (Porac, Thomas, Wilson, Paton, & Kanfer, 1995; White, 1981). While most early studies of market categories have treated them as stable and focused on their constraining and disciplinary functions (Zuckerman, 1999), scholars have started to examine market category dynamics, e.g., how new market categories emerge (Durand & Khaire, 2017; Kennedy & Fiss, 2013; Khaire & Wadhwani, 2010; Navis & Glynn, 2010; Rao et al., 2003), how market categories evolve (Rao et al., 2005; Ruef & Patterson, 2009), and how market categories decline (Navis et al., 2012). Lo and colleagues (2020: 85) later proposed that although past studies have examined the emergence and decline of categories as different processes, they can be conceptualized as "two ends of a thread defined by a single important question: What makes a category more or less viable?" Category viability is defined by Lo et al. (2020: 86) as "a category's ability (1) to group similar entities and differentiate between dissimilar ones and (2) to facilitate exchange and coordination between actors." Following this definition, category viability captures the degree to which a market category is current and useful in conveying meaning, shaping sensemaking, and acting as an interface for exchange and coordination among diverse actors.

While past studies have not used the term "category viability," they have offered important, yet competing, insights regarding what contribute to category viability. Some studies have suggested that for a category to be viable, it needs have a clearly delineated boundary and distinct identity (e.g., McKendrick, Jaffee, Carroll, & Khessina, 2003; Rao et al., 2003) and initially disparate actions and meanings need to converge for a category to successfully emerge and sustain (Khaire & Wadhwani, 2010). Other studies argue instead that for a category to be viable, it needs to allow a certain level of ambiguity and interpretive flexibility so as to attract and accommodate a diverse set of members, enable category growth, and enhance its robustness (e.g., Pontikes & Barnett, 2015; Wry, Lounsbury, & Glynn, 2011).

Lo et al. (2020) reconciled these competing views by acknowledging both sides of the argument and emphasizing a category's balanced position in terms of both coherence and distinctiveness. Category coherence refers to the perceived association and resemblance among the entities that constitute a category's membership (Rosch & Mervis, 1975). When category coherence is high, the category has a sharper boundary, resemblance among members is high, and a clear prototype exists, all of which help reduce cognitive burden of audiences in identifying and maintaining category boundaries (Hannan et al., 2007; Negro et al., 2011). However, when category coherence is overly high, it "comes at the cost of rendering the category both rigid and narrow, making it less useful for facilitating exchange and coordination" (Lo et al., 2020: 90). Category distinctiveness reflects the relative position of a category in the broader classification and meaning system and captures the degree to which the category overlaps with other categories in the system (Lo et al., 2020). A category needs to be sufficiently distinct from other categories in the system to be useful as a standalone category and at the same time, not too distant from other categories to avoid failing to be recognized as part of the classification system.

Accordingly, category viability is a delicate balancing act in terms of both coherence and distinctiveness at both the organization and category levels. As Lo et al. (2020: 94–5) cogently argued:

> [C]category members may actively engage in the shaping and re(positioning) of the category they are affiliated with. Indeed, deliberate actions and reactions of interested actors may change the internal composition or external relations of a category, which, in turn, will shape the viability of a category as well as its adjacent categories, influencing category dynamics in complex ways. Distinctiveness and coherence are neither fixed nor inherent properties of any category on its own, since they can change both with shifts in their own members and features and with shifts in those of other categories and in the relative positioning among categories. In other words, we see the formation and change of categories and social ontologies as a recursive and continuous process that is too complex to fit a unidirectional causal statement.

Scholars have only recently started to engage these insights in empirical studies and examine optimal distinctiveness at the market category level. A notable example is Tracey, Dalpiaz, and Phillips' (2018) qualitative case study of H-Farm, a type of busines incubator in Italy, in which the authors conceptualized the emergence and development of this market category as an ongoing optimal distinctiveness work. H-Farm is an Italian venture founded in 2005 that combines seed incubation, venture capital (VC) investment, education, and consulting in the digital, web, and new media industries. H-Farm represents a new market category in the Italian context that resembles the business incubator type of organizations that originated in Silicon Valley. At the founding of H-Farm, private for-profit incubators were nonexistent in Italy, and thus the business incubator as a market category was almost "a completely new reality in the country" (Tracey et al., 2018: 1633). Media coverage on this new venture and new market category was scattered, a robust VC sector was lacking to support its graduating firms, and the whole entrepreneurial ecosystem is underdeveloped in H-Farm's local context. Therefore, in founding H-Farm, entrepreneurs need not just to overcome the liability of newness of this specific organization but also to establish the legitimacy and distinctiveness of business incubator as a market category translated from a foreign context.

Using data collected through interviews, archival records, and field observations and meetings, Tracey et al. (2018) uncovered the changing legitimacy and differentiation pressures entrepreneurs faced as they created H-Farm by translating an existing organizational form from an institutional context very different from their own. According to the authors, the translation experienced three phases. In the first phase of the translation, entrepreneurs immediately faced questions from local-level stakeholders (e.g., local prospective entrepreneurs, domestic investors, policy makers) about the legitimacy of the new venture and the new organizational form. To address this legitimacy challenge, entrepreneurs engaged local-level authentication work to explain the venture to local-level stakeholders and adjust the model to the local context to fit with local expectations. The legitimacy challenge from local-level stakeholders also motivated entrepreneurs to acquire resources outside of their locale and seek approval from global category-level stakeholders (e.g., international entrepreneurs, international VCs, high-profile accelerators in the US). As such, in the second phase, entrepreneurs needed to signal and explain their venture's conformity to category-level stakeholders' expectations. Finally, in the third phase, as local rivals emerged and increasingly competed for local resources, H-Farm faced an increasing pressure to differentiate from local rivals to stand out. Similarly, at the category level, as the business incubator category became more prevalent across different institutional contexts, H-Farm and the Italian business incubator category needed to respond by not just conforming to category-level expectations but also differentiating from international rivals to signal uniqueness and distinction. Overall, the emergence and evolution of H-Farm and of the Italian business incubator category more generally can be viewed as a process of "dual optimal distinctiveness work," which involved entrepreneurs' engagement of both practice and meaning work (in other words, both practical and symbolic actions) to manage the changing nature and strengths of legitimacy and competitive pressures and meet the expectations of local and international stakeholders.

Tracey et al. (2018) is an exemplary study of how the optimal distinctiveness orienting framework can be extended from the organization to the market category level, and how qualitative research can play an important role in further unleashing the power of optimal distinctiveness scholarship. Future research can build on this pioneering work and explore how the four key aspects of the orienting framework can inform and enrich the growing body of research on market category dynamics. More research is needed on how optimal distinctiveness dynamics play out not just in the emerging and growing stages of market categories but also in stages of category settlement and decline. Would optimal distinctiveness be a stronger or weaker imperative across these different stages of category evolution? How would the nature and intensity of legitimacy and competitive pressures shift over time? What constitute an optimally distinct positioning strategy in declining market categories? What is the most relevant benchmark for gauging optimal distinctiveness in the decline stage? To take this chain of thought one step further, whether and how does optimal distinctiveness play a role in the reemergence and revitalization of legacy market categories (Raffaelli, 2019)? These questions present great opportunities for future research.

7 Conclusion

It has been nearly three decades since Brewer (1991) pioneered optimal distinctiveness research in social psychology and more than two decades since Deephouse (1999) extended the idea to the organizational level to propose strategic balance theory. Although it is a stretch to claim that strategic balance theory has developed into a robust and distinct research paradigm, the central theme it concerns with – the conformity versus differentiation tension – underpins much of the research that sits at the intersection of strategic management and organization theory (Zhao et al., 2017). This tension has provided a rare platform for strategic management scholars and organization theorists to engage each other directly, who often "barely acknowledge each other's existence" (Davis & DeWitt, 2021: 2). The same theme has also attracted attention and stimulated interest among entrepreneurship and international business scholars (Lounsbury & Glynn, 2001, 2019; McKnight & Zietsma, 2018; Pant & Ramachandran, 2017; Younger & Fisher, 2020). This clearly signals the broad relevance and appeal of the notion of optimal distinctiveness in general management scholarship. Without an orienting conceptual framework, however, scholars embedded in these different research domains have mostly worked in isolation, adopted different languages, and employed varied conceptual terms and operationalizations in addressing essentially the same question. As a result, there is still a lack of consensus in optimal distinctiveness research, and optimal distinctiveness is often evoked as a companion to other organization theories rather than as a standalone theory by itself.

Writing this Element afforded me the opportunity to build on and extend the burgeoning literature on optimal distinctiveness and allowed me to further categorize and synthesize contemporary optimal distinctiveness research. Major themes in contemporary macro-level studies of optimal distinctiveness are uncovered and organized into an orienting conceptual framework that I hope can guide future research on this important topic. By discussing the implications of this orienting framework for research in various disciplines, such as strategy, entrepreneurship, and international business, I also tried to highlight potentially productive intersections between optimal distinctiveness and these scholarly domains and establish intellectual linkages among otherwise isolated researchers. Furthermore, I concretized the value of the orienting framework by focusing on one particular research topic – competitive positioning of organizations – and used four empirical examples to demonstrate its promise in guiding empirical research. Finally, I discussed the opportunity to apply the orienting framework to different levels of analysis beyond organizations, in particular to the study of emergence, development, and decline of market categories.

All these efforts are necessary steps to show the real potential of optimal distinctiveness beyond being simply a broad umbrella concept – that is, a broad concept or idea that encompasses and accounts for a diverse set of phenomena (Hirsch & Levin, 1999). In fact, even the view of optimal distinctiveness as an umbrella concept does not diminish its value in either scholarly or practitioner communities. Such umbrella concepts are "necessary to keep the field relevant and in touch with the larger, albeit messier, world" (Hirsch & Levin, 1999: 200). At the same time, I also believe that a certain level of validity and reliability needs to be reached in order to make sure studies of optimal distinctiveness are not sloppy or overly scattered. The time is ripe for the optimal distinctiveness literature to be subject to both advocacy and policing and to strike a rough balance between openness and discipline (March, 1996; Pfeffer, 1993).

To this end, scholars need to be aware that focusing on certain elements of the orienting framework, such as multidimensionality and contextual contingencies, can lead to ad hoc and noncumulative empirical studies in which optimal distinctiveness is idiosyncratically defined and measured and researchers focus on different organizational dimensions and heterogeneous contextual factors. As the body of optimal distinctiveness research continues to grow along these lines, further validity policing work is needed to sort out the most and the least relevant organizational dimensions that contribute to optimal distinctiveness, specific configurations of organizational dimensions that stand out as the most or the least effective, the applicability and fit of these configurations with different types of environment, and more fundamentally, the motivation and selection behind each organization's positioning strategies and their unique trajectories toward either a global or local optimal distinctiveness.

Similarly, as the orienting framework of optimal distinctiveness implies, what constitutes optimal distinctiveness also hinges upon the audiences making the evaluations and the specific lenses and benchmarks they use. As such, optimal distinctiveness is essentially a value-based concept, and there is no universally agreeable optimally positioning strategy that matches all audience expectations. This heterogeneity of audience expectations regarding what optimal distinctiveness means and what it entails may lead scholars to think that reaching consensus in optimal distinctiveness research is an impossible or futile effort. There might even be arguments for a halt in or pull back of studies of optimal distinctiveness, especially among those validity police who are less tolerant of conceptual complexity and ambiguity.

While these are valid concerns and calls for discipline, it is equally important to keep an open mind. Conceptual complexity and ambiguity can be generative and should thus be embraced, especially at this stage of development of optimal distinctiveness research. Attending to multidimensionality, uncovering contextual contingencies, tracing temporal dynamics, identifying the most relevant audiences in optimal distinctiveness evaluations, and clarifying the diverse audience expectations are all critically important not just for advancing theory but also for advising managers and entrepreneurs as they navigate industry and market environments characterized as multiplex, fragmented, and dynamic with increasingly complex stakeholder relationships and expectations.

References

Abrahamson, E. 1991. Managerial fads and fashions: The diffusion and rejection of innovations. *Academy of Management Review*, 16(3), pp. 586–612.

Agrawal, A., Gans, J., & Goldfarb, A. 2018. *Prediction machines: The simple economics of artificial intelligence.* Cambridge, MA : Harvard Business Review Press.

Aguilera, R. V., Judge, W. Q., & Terjesen, S. A. 2018. Corporate governance deviance. *Academy of Management Review*, 43(1), pp. 87–109.

Amit, R., Brander, J., & Zott, C. 1998. Why do venture capital firms exist? Theory and Canadian evidence. *Journal of Business Venturing*, 13(6), pp. 441–66.

Aoyama, Y. & Izushi, H. 2003. Hardware gimmick or cultural innovation? Technological, cultural, and social foundations of the Japanese video game industry. *Research Policy*, 32(3), pp. 423–44.

Arsenault, D. 2009. Video game genre, evolution and innovation. *Journal for Computer Game Culture*, 3(2), pp. 149–76.

Askin, N. & Mauskapf, M. 2017. What makes popular culture popular? Product features and optimal differentiation in music. *American Sociological Review*, 82(5), pp. 910–44.

Baker, T. & Nelson, R. E. 2005. Creating something from nothing: Resource construction through entrepreneurial bricolage. *Administrative Science Quarterly*, 50(3), pp. 329–66.

Bansal, P. 2003. From issues to actions: The importance of individual concerns and organizational values in responding to natural environmental issues. *Organization Science*, 14(5), pp. 510–27.

Barlow, M. A., Verhaal, J. C., & Angus, R. W. 2019. Optimal distinctiveness, strategic categorization, and product market entry on the Google Play app platform. *Strategic Management Journal*, 40(8), pp. 1219–42.

Barney, J. 1991. Firm resources and sustained competitive advantage. *Journal of Management*, 17(1), pp. 99–120.

Bartlett, C. A. & Ghoshal, S. 1989. *Managing across borders: The transnational solution.* Cambridge, MA: Harvard Business Press.

Baum, J. A. C., Li, S. X., & Usher, J. M. 2000. Making the next move: How experiential and vicarious learning shape the locations of chains' acquisitions. *Administrative Science Quarterly*, 45(4), pp. 766–801.

Bayus, B. L. & Shankar, V. 2003. Network effects and competition: An empirical analysis of the home video game industry. *Strategic Management Journal*, 24(4), pp. 375–84.

Bazerman, M. H. 2005. Conducting influential research: The need for prescriptive implications. *Academy of Management Review*, 30(1): 25–31.

Benninga, S. & Sarig, O. 1997. *Corporate finance: A valuation approach.* New York: McGraw-Hill.

Beunza, D. & Garud, R. 2007. Calculators, lemmings or frame-makers? The intermediary role of securities analysts. *Sociological Review*, 55, pp. 13–39.

Birkinshaw, J. & Gupta, K. 2013. Clarifying the distinctive contribution of ambidexterity to the field of organization studies. *Academy of Management Perspectives*, 27(4), pp. 287–98.

Boulongne, R. & Durand, R. 2021. Evaluating ambiguous offerings. *Organization Science*, 32(2), pp. 257–72.

Bowers, A. 2015. Relative comparison and category membership: The case of equity analysts. *Organization Science*, 26(2), pp. 571–83.

Bowers, A. 2020. Balanced but not fair: Strategic balancing, rating allocations, and third-party intermediaries. *Strategic Organization*, 18(3), pp. 427–47.

Bowers, A. & Prato, M. 2019. The role of third-party rankings in status dynamics: How does the stability of rankings induce status changes? *Organization Science*, 30(6), pp. 1146–64.

Brauer, M. & Wiersema, M. 2018. Analyzing analyst research: A review of past coverage and recommendations for future research. *Journal of Management*, 44(1), pp. 218–48.

Brewer, M. B. 1991. The social self: On being the same and different at the same time. *Personality and Social Psychology Bulletin*, 17(5), pp. 475–82.

Brewer, M. B. & Silver, M. D. 2000. Group distinctiveness, social identification, and collective mobilization. *Self, Identity, and Social Movements*, 13, pp. 153–71.

Brown, S. L. & Eisenhardt, K. M. 1997. The art of continuous change: Linking complexity theory and time-paced evolution in relentlessly shifting organizations. *Administrative Science Quarterly*, 42(1), pp. 1–34.

Bu, J., Zhao, E. Y., Li, K., & Li, J. M. 2022. Multilevel optimal distinctiveness: Examining the impact of within- and between-organization distinctiveness of product design on market performance. *Strategic Management Journal*, forthcoming.

Buhr, H., Funk, R. J., & Owen-Smith, J. 2021. The authenticity premium: Balancing conformity and innovation in high technology industries. *Research Policy*, 50(1), pp. 1–21.

Capron, L. & Mitchell, W. 2012. *Build, borrow, or buy: Solving the growth dilemma.* Boston, MA: Harvard Business Press.

Cattani, G., Dunbar, R. L. M., & Shapira, Z. 2017. How commitment to craftsmanship leads to unique value: Steinway & Sons' differentiation strategy. *Strategy Science*, 2(1), pp. 13–38.

Cattani, G., Ferriani, S., Negro, G., & Perretti, F. 2008. The structure of consensus: Network ties, legitimation, and exit rates of US feature film producer organizations. *Administrative Science Quarterly*, 53(1), pp. 145–82.

Cattani, G., Porac, J. F., & Thomas, H. 2017. Categories and competition. *Strategic Management Journal*, 38(1), pp. 64–92.

Caves, R. E. & Porter, M. E. 1977. From entry barriers to mobility barriers: Conjectural decisions and contrived deterrence to new competition. *Quarterly Journal of Economics*, 91(2), pp. 241–61.

Cennamo, C. & Santalo, J. 2013. Platform competition: Strategic trade-offs in platform markets. *Strategic Management Journal*, 34(11), pp. 1331–50.

Chan, T. H., Lee, Y. G., & Jung, H. 2021. Anchored differentiation: The role of temporal distance in the comparison and evaluation of new product designs. *Organization Science*, 32(6), pp. 1523–41.

Chatterji, A. K., Findley, M., Jensen, N. M., Meier, S., & Nielson, D. 2016. Field experiments in strategy research. *Strategic Management Journal*, 37, pp. 116–32.

Chen, M.-J. & Hambrick, D. C. 1995. Speed, stealth, and selective attack: How small firms differ from large firms in competitive behavior. *Academy of Management Journal*, 38(2), pp. 453–82.

Chen, M.-J. & Miller, D. 2012. Competitive dynamics: Themes, trends, and a prospective research platform. *Academy of Management Annals*, 6(1), pp. 135–210.

Child, J. 1972. Organization structure and strategies of control: A replication of the Aston study. *Administrative Science Quarterly*, 17(2), pp. 163–77.

Clements, M. T. & Ohashi, H. 2005. Indirect network effects and the product cycle: Video games in the U.S., 1994–2002. *Journal of Industrial Economics*, 53(4), pp. 515–42.

Cobb, J. A., Wry, T., & Zhao, E. Y. 2016. Funding financial inclusion: Institutional logics and the contextual contingency of funding for microfinance organizations. *Academy of Management Journal*, 59(6), pp. 2103–31.

Conger, M., Mcmullen, J. S., Bergman, B. J., & York, J. G. 2018. Category membership, identity control, and the reevaluation of prosocial opportunities. *Journal of Business Venturing*, 33(2), pp. 179–206.

Davis, G. F. & DeWitt, T. 2021. Organization theory and the resource-based view of the firm: The great divide. *Journal of Management*, 47(7), pp. 1684–97.

Day, G. S. 1981. Strategic market analysis and definition: An integrated approach. *Strategic Management Journal*, 2(3), pp. 281–99.

Dayin, L. 2007. The Elder Scrolls IV: Oblivion. www.mobygames.com/game/xbox360/elder-scrolls-iv-oblivion/reviews/reviewerId,89605/. Accessed August 24, 2020.

Deephouse, D. L. 1996. Does isomorphism legitimate? *Academy of Management Journal*, 39(4), pp. 1024–39.

Deephouse, D. L. 1999. To be different, or to be the same? It's a question (and theory) of strategic balance. *Strategic Management Journal*, 20(2), pp. 147–66.

Deephouse, D. L., Bundy, J., Tost, L. P., & Suchman, M. C. 2017. Organizational legitimacy: Six key questions. In Greenwood, R., Oliver, C., Lawrence, T. B., & Meyer, R. E. (eds.). *The SAGE handbook of organizational institutionalism*. London: SAGE, pp. 27–54.

Delery, J. E. & Doty, D. H. 1996. Modes of theorizing in strategic human resource management: Tests of universalistic, contingency, and configurational performance predictions. *Academy of Management Journal*, 39(4), pp. 802–35.

Delios, A., Gaur, A. S., & Makino, S. 2008. The timing of international expansion: Information, rivalry and imitation among Japanese firms, 1980–2002. *Journal of Management Studies*, 45(1), pp. 169–95.

DesJardine, M. R. & Durand, R. 2020. Disentangling the effects of hedge fund activism on firm financial and social performance. *Strategic Management Journal*, 41, pp. 1054–82.

DiMaggio, P. J. & Powell, W. W. 1983. The iron cage revisited: Institutional isomorphism and collective rationality in organizational fields. *American Sociological Review*, 48(2), pp. 147–60.

DiMaggio, P. J. & Powell, W. W. 1991. *The new institutionalism in organizational analysis*. Chicago, IL: University of Chicago Press.

Dranove, D., Peteraf, M., & Shanley, M. 1998. Do strategic groups exist? An economic framework for analysis. *Strategic Management Journal*, 19(11), pp. 1029–44.

Durand, R. & Haans, R. 2021. Optimal distinctiveness, seriously? Unanswered questions – theoretical and methodological hints. HEC Paris Working Paper.

Durand, R. & Jourdan, J. 2012. Jules or Jim: Alternative conformity to minority logics. *Academy of Management Journal*, 55(6), pp. 1295–315.

Durand, R. & Khaire, M. 2017. Where do market categories come from and how? Distinguishing category creation from category emergence. *Journal of Management*, 43(1), pp. 87–110.

Durand, R. & Kremp, P. A. 2016. Classical deviation: Organizational and individual status as antecedents of conformity. *Academy of Management Journal*, 59(1), pp. 65–89.

Durand, R. & Paolella, L. 2013. Category stretching: Reorienting research on categories in strategy, entrepreneurship, and organization theory. *Journal of Management Studies*, 50(6), pp. 1100–23.

Durand, R., Rao, H., & Monin, P. 2007. Code and conduct in French cuisine: Impact of code changes on external evaluations. *Strategic Management Journal*, 28(5), pp. 455–72.

Durand, R., Szostak, B., Jourdan, J., & Thornton, P. H. 2013. Institutional logics as strategic resources. In Lounsbury, M. (ed.). *Research in the sociology of organizations*. Bingley, UK: Emerald, pp. 165–201.

Fama, E. F. 1965. The behavior of stock-market prices. *Journal of Business*, 38 (1), pp. 34–105.

Farjoun, M., Smith, W., Langley, A., & Tsoukas, H. 2018. *Dualities, dialectics, and paradoxes in organizational life*. Oxford: Oxford University Press.

Feldman, E. R. 2016. Corporate spinoffs and analysts' coverage decisions: The implications for diversified firms. *Strategic Management Journal*, 37(7), pp. 1196–219.

Finkelstein, S. & Hambrick, D. C. 1990. Top-management-team tenure and organizational outcomes: The moderating role of managerial discretion. *Administrative Science Quarterly*, 35(3), pp. 484–503.

Fisher, G., Kotha, S., & Lahiri, A. 2016. Changing with the times: An integrated view of identity, legitimacy, and new venture life cycles. *Academy of Management Review*, 41(3), pp. 383–409.

Fiss, P. C. 2007. A set-theoretic approach to organizational configurations. *Academy of Management Review*, 32(4), pp. 1180–98.

Fiss, P. C. 2011. Building better causal theories: A fuzzy set approach to typologies in organization research. *Academy of Management Journal*, 54 (2), pp. 393–420.

Friedland, R. & Alford, R. 1991. Bringing society back in: Symbols, practices and institutional contradictions. In Powell, W. W. & DiMaggio, P. J. (eds.). *The new institutionalism in organizational analysis*. Chicago, IL: University of Chicago Press, pp. 232–63.

Fromkin, H. L. & Snyder, C. R. 1980. The search for uniqueness and valuation of scarcity. In Gergen, K. J. et al. (eds.). *Social exchange*. New York : Plenum Press, pp. 57–75.

Garud, R., Jain, S., & Kumaraswamy, A. 2002. Institutional entrepreneurship in the sponsorship of common technological standards: The case of Sun Microsystems and Java. *Academy of Management Journal*, 45, pp. 196–214.

Garud, R., Lant, T. K., & Schildt, H. A. 2019. Generative imitation, strategic distancing and optimal distinctiveness during the growth, decline and stabilization of Silicon Alley. *Innovation: Organization & Management*, 21 (1), pp. 187–213.

Ge, J. & Micelotta, E. 2019. When does the family matter? Institutional pressures and corporate philanthropy in China. *Organization Studies*, 40(6), pp. 833–57.

Gehman, J. & Grimes, M. 2017. Hidden badge of honor: How contextual distinctiveness affects category promotion among certified B corporations. *Academy of Management Journal*, 60(6), pp. 2294–320.

Gehman, J. & Soublière, J. F. 2017. Cultural entrepreneurship: From making culture to cultural making. *Innovation*, 19(1), pp. 61–73.

Giddens, A. 1979. *Central problems in social theory: Action, structure and contradiction in social analysis*. Berkeley & Los Angeles: University of California Press.

Gimeno, J., Hoskisson, R. E., Beal, B. D., & Wan, W. P. 2005. Explaining the clustering of international expansion moves: A critical test in the U.S. telecommunications industry. *Academy of Management Journal*, 48 (2), pp. 297–319.

Glaser, V. L., Krikorian Atkinson, M., & Fiss, P. C. 2020. Goal-based categorization: Dynamic classification in the display advertising industry. *Organization Studies*, 41(7), pp. 921–43.

Glynn, M. A. & Abzug, R. 1998. Isomorphism and competitive differentiation in the organizational name game. *Advances in Strategic Management*, 15, pp. 105–28.

Glynn, M. A. & Abzug, R. 2002. Institutionalizing identity: Symbolic isomorphism and organizational names. *Academy of Management Journal*, 45 (1), pp. 267–80.

Goldenstein, J., Hunoldt, M., & Oertel, S. 2019. How optimal distinctiveness affects new ventures' failure risk: A contingency perspective. *Journal of Business Venturing*, 34(3), pp. 477–95.

Goldstone, R. L. 1994. The role of similarity in categorization: Providing a groundwork. *Cognition*, 52(2), pp. 125–57.

Granqvist, N., Grodal, S., & Woolley, J. L. 2013. Hedging your bets: Explaining executives' market labeling strategies in nanotechnology. *Organization Science*, 24(2), pp. 395–413.

Greenwood, R., Raynard, M., Kodeih, F., Micelotta, E. R., & Lounsbury, M. 2011. Institutional complexity and organizational responses. *Academy of Management Annals*, 5(1), pp. 317–71.

Greenwood, R. & Suddaby, R. 2006. Institutional entrepreneurship in mature fields: The big five accounting firms. *Academy of Management Journal*, 49, pp. 27–48.

Grimes, M. G. 2018. The pivot: How founders respond to feedback through idea and identity work. *Academy of Management Journal*, 61(5), pp. 1692–717.

Gupta, K., Crilly, D., & Greckhamer, T. 2020. Stakeholder engagement strategies, national institutions, and firm performance: A configurational perspective. *Strategic Management Journal*, 41(10), pp. 1869–900.

Haans, R. F. 2019. What's the value of being different when everyone is? The effects of distinctiveness on performance in homogeneous versus heterogeneous categories. *Strategic Management Journal*, 40(1), pp. 3–27.

Hahl O. & Ha J. 2019. Committed diversification: Why authenticity insulates against penalties for diversification. Organization *Science* 31(1), pp. 1–22.

Hamid, H., O'Kane, C., & Everett André, M. 2019. Conforming to the host country versus being distinct to our home countries: Ethnic migrant entrepreneurs' identity work in cross-cultural settings. *International Journal of Entrepreneurial Behavior & Research*, 25(5), pp. 919–35.

Hamilton, B. H. & Nickerson, J. A. (2003). Correcting for endogeneity in strategic management research. *Strategic Organization*, 1, pp. 51–78.

Hannan, M. T. & Freeman, J. 1977. The population ecology of organizations. *American Journal of Sociology*, 82(5), pp. 929–64.

Hannan, M. T., Pólos, L., & Carroll, G. R. 2007. *Logics of organization theory: Audiences, codes, and ecologies*. Princeton, NJ: Princeton University Press.

Hannigan, T. R., Haans, R. F. J., Vakili, K., Tchalian, H., Glaser, V. L., Wang, M. S. et al. 2019. Topic modeling in management research: Rendering new theory from textual data. *Academy of Management Annals*, 13(2), pp. 586–632.

Higgins, E. T. & Bargh, J. A. 1987. Social cognition and social perception. *Annual Review of Psychology*, 38(1), pp. 369–425.

Hinings, C. R. & Greenwood, R. 1988. The normative prescription of organizations. In Zucker, L. G. (ed.). *Institutional patterns and organizations: Culture and environment*. Cambridge, MA: Ballinger, pp. 53–70.

Hirsch, P. M. & Levin, D. Z. 1999. Umbrella advocates versus validity police: A life-cycle model. *Organization Science*, 10(2), pp. 199–212.

Hsu, G. & Grodal, S. 2015. Category taken-for-grantedness as a strategic opportunity: The case of light cigarettes, 1964 to 1993. *American Sociological Review*, 80(1), pp. 28–62.

Ingram, P. & Yue, L. Q. 2008. Structure, affect and identity as bases of organizational competition and cooperation. *Academy of Management Annals*, 2(1), pp. 275–303.

Jennings, J. E., Jennings, P. D., & Greenwood, R. 2009. Novelty and new firm performance: The case of employment systems in knowledge-intensive service organizations. *Journal of Business Venturing*, 24(4), pp. 338–59.

Jensen, M. 2004. Who gets Wall Street's attention? How alliance announcements and alliance density affect analyst coverage. *Strategic Organization*, 2 (3), pp. 293–312.

Jourdan, J. 2018. Institutional specialization and survival: Theory and evidence from the French film industry. *Strategy Science*, 3(2), pp. 408–25.

Kennedy, M. T. & Fiss, P. C. 2013. An ontological turn in categories research: From standards of legitimacy to evidence of actuality. *Journal of Management Studies*, 50, pp. 1138–54.

Khaire, M. & Wadhwani, R. D. 2010. Changing landscapes: The construction of meaning and value in a new market category – Modern Indian art. *Academy of Management Journal*, 53(6), pp. 1281–304.

Khanna, T. & Palepu, K. 2000. The future of business groups in emerging markets: Long-run evidence from Chile. *Academy of Management Journal*, 43(3), pp. 268–85.

Khessina, O. M., Reis, S., & Verhaal, J. C. 2020. Stepping out of the shadows: Identity exposure as a remedy for stigma transfer concerns in the medical marijuana market. *Administrative Science Quarterly*, 66(3), pp. 569–611.

Klepper, S. & Simons, K. L. 2000. Dominance by birthright: Entry of prior radio producers and competitive ramifications in the U.S. television receiver industry. *Strategic Management Journal*, 21(10–11), pp. 997–1016.

Kostova, T. & Zaheer, S. 1999. Organizational legitimacy under conditions of complexity: The case of the multinational enterprise. *Academy of Management Review*, 24(1), pp. 64–81.

Lambkin, M. & Day, G. S. 1989. Evolutionary processes in competitive markets: Beyond the product life cycle. *Journal of Marketing*, 53(3), pp. 4–20.

Lawrence, T. & Suddaby, R. 2006. Institutions and institutional work. In Clegg, S. R., Hardy, C., Lawrence, T. B., & Nord, W. R. (ed.). *Handbook of organization studies*, 2nd ed.. London: SAGE, pp. 215–54.

Lawrence, T., Suddaby, R., & Leca, B. 2011. Institutional work: Refocusing institutional studies of organization. *Journal of Management Inquiry*, 20(1): 52–8.

Leonardelli, G. J., Pickett, C. L., & Brewer, M. B. 2010. Optimal distinctiveness theory: A framework for social identity, social cognition, and intergroup relations. In Zanna, M. P. & Olson, J. M. (eds.). *Advances in experimental social psychology*. Cambridge, MA: Academic Press, pp. 63–113.

Lieberman, M. B. & Asaba, S. 2006. Why do firms imitate each other? *Academy of Management Review*, 31(2), pp. 366–85.

Lingo, E. L. & O'Mahony, S. 2010. Nexus work: Brokerage on creative projects. *Administrative Science Quarterly*, 55(1), pp. 47–81.

Litov, L. P., Moreton, P., & Zenger, T. R. 2012. Corporate strategy, analyst coverage, and the uniqueness paradox. *Management Science*, 58(10), pp. 1797–815.

Lo, J., Fiss, P. C., Rhee, E. Y., & Kennedy, M. T. 2020. Category viability: Balanced levels of coherence and distinctiveness. *Academy of Management Review*, 45(1), pp. 85–108.

Loguidice, B. & Barton, M. 2009. *Vintage games: An insider look at the history of Grand Theft Auto, Super Mario, and the most influential games of all time.* Burlington, MA: Focal Press.

Lounsbury, M. & Glynn, M. A. 2001. Cultural entrepreneurship: Stories, legitimacy, and the acquisition of resources. *Strategic Management Journal*, 22(6–7), pp. 545–64.

Lounsbury, M. & Glynn, M. A. 2019. *Cultural entrepreneurship: A new agenda for the study of entrepreneurial processes and possibilities.* Cambridge: Cambridge University Press.

Lounsbury, M. & Rao, H. 2004. Sources of durability and change in market classifications: A study of the reconstitution of product categories in the American mutual fund industry, 1944–1985. *Social Forces*, 82(3), pp. 969–99.

Luo, Y., Zhang, H., & Bu, J. 2019. Developed country MNEs investing in developing economies: Progress and prospect. *Journal of International Business Studies*, 50(4), pp. 633–67.

Luscher, L. S. & Lewis, M. W. 2008. Organizational change and managerial sensemaking: Working through paradox. *Academy of Management Journal*, 51(2), pp. 221–40.

Madsen, T. L. & Walker, G. (2015). *Modern competitive strategy.* New York: McGraw-Hill.

Maguire, S., Hardy, C., & Lawrence, T. B. 2004. Institutional entrepreneurship in emerging fields: HIV/AIDS treatment advocacy in Canada. *Academy of Management Journal*, 47, 657–79.

Majzoubi, M., Zhao, E. Y., Zuzul, T., & Fisher, G. 2021. Optimal distinctiveness in dual benchmark settings: Effects of exemplar similarity and firm typicality on audience evaluation. Working Paper.

March, J. G. 1996. Continuity and change in theories of organizational action. *Administrative Science Quarterly*, 41, pp. 278–87.

Markus, H. R. & Kitayama, S. 1991. Culture and the self: Implications for cognition, emotion, and motivation. *Psychological Review*, 98(2), pp. 224–53.

Martens, M. L., Jennings, J. E., & Jennings, P. D. 2007. Do the stories they tell get them the money they need? The role of entrepreneurial narratives in resource acquisition. *Academy of Management Journal*, 50(5), pp. 1107–32.

Maslach, C. 1974. Social and personal bases of individuation. *Journal of Personality and Social Psychology*, 29(3), pp. 411–25.

Mathias, B. D., Huyghe, A., Frid, C. J., & Galloway, T. L. 2018. An identity perspective on coopetition in the craft beer industry. *Strategic Management Journal*, 39(12), pp. 3086–115.

McDonald, R. M. & Eisenhardt, K. M. 2020. Parallel play: Startups, nascent markets, and effective business-model design. *Administrative Science Quarterly*, 65(2), pp. 483–523.

McGee, J. & Thomas, H. 1986. Strategic groups: Theory, research and taxonomy. *Strategic Management Journal*, 7(2), pp. 141–60.

McKendrick, D. G., Jaffee, J., Carroll, G. R., & Khessina, O. 2003. In the bud? Analysis of disk array producers as a (possibly) emergent organizational form. *Administrative Science Quarterly*, 48, pp. 60–93.

McKnight, B. & Zietsma, C. 2018. Finding the threshold: A configurational approach to optimal distinctiveness. *Journal of Business Venturing*, 33(4), pp. 493–512.

Mcphee, R. & Poole, M. 2001. Organizational structures and configurations. In Jablin, F. M. & Putnam, L. L. (eds.). *The new handbook of organizational communication*. Thousand Oaks, CA: SAGE, pp. 503–43.

Meitner, M. 2006. *The market approach to comparable company valuation*, vol. 35. New York: Springer Science & Business Media.

Meyer, A. D., Tsui, A. S., & Hinings, C. R. 1993. Configurational approaches to organizational analysis. *Academy of Management Journal*, 36(6), pp. 1175–95.

Meyer, J. W. & Rowan, B. 1977. Institutionalized organizations: Formal structure as myth and ceremony. *American Journal of Sociology*, 83(2), pp.340–63.

Micelotta, E., Washington, M., & Docekalova, I. 2018. Industry gender imprinting and new venture creation: The liabilities of women's leagues in the sports industry. *Entrepreneurship Theory and Practice*, 42(1), pp. 94–128.

Miles, R. E. & Snow, C. C. 1978. *Organizational strategy, structure, and process*. New York: McGraw-Hill.

Miller, D. 1996. Configurations revisited. *Strategic Management Journal*, 17 (7), pp. 505–12.

Miller, D., Amore, M. D., Le Breton-Miller, I., Minichilli, A., & Quarato, F. 2018. Strategic distinctiveness in family firms: Firm institutional heterogeneity and configurational multidimensionality. *Journal of Family Business Strategy*, 9(1), pp. 16–26.

Miller, D., Le Breton-Miller, I., & Lester, R. H. 2013. Family firm governance, strategic conformity, and performance: Institutional vs. strategic perspectives. *Organization Science*, 24(1), pp. 189–209.

Miller, M. H. & Modigliani, F. 1961. Dividend policy, growth, and the valuation of shares. *Journal of Business*, 34(4), pp. 411–33.

Miller, S. R., Indro, D. C., Richards, M., & Chng, D. H. M. 2013. Financial implications of local and nonlocal rival isomorphism: A signaling paradox. *Journal of Management*, 39(7), pp. 1979–2008.

Mintzberg, H. 1983. *Structures in five: Designing effective organizations*. Englewood Cliffs, NJ: Prentice-Hall.

Misangyi, V. F., Greckhamer, T., Furnari, S. et al. 2017. Embracing causal complexity: The emergence of a neo-configurational perspective. *Journal of Management*, 43(1), pp. 255–82.

Mitchell, R. K., Agle, B. R., & Wood, D. J. 1997. Toward a theory of stakeholder identification and salience: Defining the principle of who and what really counts. *Academy of Management Review*, 22(4), pp. 853–86.

Mollick, E. 2012. People and process, suits and innovators: The role of individuals in firm performance. *Strategic Management Journal*, 33(9), pp. 1001–15.

Mullainathan, S. & Spiess, J. 2017. Machine learning: An applied econometric approach. *Journal of Economic Perspectives*, 31(2), pp. 87–106.

Murphy, G. L. & Medin, D. L. 1985. The role of theories in conceptual coherence. *Psychological Review*, 92(3), p. 289.

Nason, R. S. & Wiklund, J. 2018. An assessment of resource-based theorizing on firm growth and suggestions for the future. *Journal of Management*, 44(1), pp. 32–60.

Navis, C., Fisher, G., Raffaelli, R., Glynn, M. A., & Watkiss, L. 2012. The market that wasn't: The non-emergence of the online grocery category. Working Paper.

Navis, C. & Glynn, M. A. 2010. How new market categories emerge: Temporal dynamics of legitimacy, identity, and entrepreneurship in satellite radio, 1990–2005. *Administrative Science Quarterly*, 55(3), pp. 439–71.

Navis, C. & Glynn, M. A. 2011. Legitimate distinctiveness and the entrepreneurial identity: Influence on investor judgments of new venture plausibility. *Academy of Management Review*, 36(3), pp. 479–99.

Negro, G., Hannan, M. T., & Rao, H. 2011. Category reinterpretation and defection: Modernism and tradition in Italian winemaking. *Organization Science*, 22, pp. 1449–63.

Nosofsky, R. M. & Johansen, M. K. 2000. Exemplar-based accounts of "multiple-system" phenomena in perceptual categorization. *Psychonomic Bulletin & Review*, 7(3), pp. 375–402.

Oehme, M. & Bort, S. 2015. SME internationalization modes in the German biotechnology industry: The influence of imitation, network position, and international experience. *Journal of International Business Studies*, 46(6), pp. 629–55.

Oliver, C. 1991. Strategic responses to institutional processes. *Academy of Management Review*, 16(1), pp. 145–79.

Oliver, C. 1997. Sustainable competitive advantage: Combining institutional and resource-based views. *Strategic Management Journal*, 18(9), pp. 697–713.

Pant, A. & Ramachandran, J. 2017. Navigating identity duality in multinational subsidiaries: A paradox lens on identity claims at Hindustan Unilever 1959–2015. *Journal of International Business Studies*, 48(6), pp. 664–92.

Paolella, L. & Durand, R. 2016. Category spanning, evaluation, and performance: Revised theory and test on the corporate law market. *Academy of Management Journal*, 59, pp. 330–51.

Peteraf, M. A. 1993. The cornerstones of competitive advantage: A resource-based view. *Strategic Management Journal*, 14(3), pp. 179–91.

Peteraf, M. A. & Barney, J. B. 2003. Unraveling the resource-based tangle. *Managerial and Decision Economics*, 24(4), pp. 309–23.

Peteraf, M. A. & Shanley, M. 1997. Getting to know you: A theory of strategic group identity. *Strategic Management Journal*, 18(1), pp. 165–86.

Pfeffer, J. 1993. Barriers to the advance of organizational science: Paradigm development as a dependent variable. *Academy of Management Review*, 18 (4), pp. 599–620.

Philippe, D. & Durand, R. 2011. The impact of norm-conforming behaviors on firm reputation. *Strategic Management Journal*, 32(9), pp. 969–93.

Pontikes, E. G. 2012. Two sides of the same coin: How ambiguous classification affects multiple audiences' evaluations. *Administrative Science Quarterly*, 57 (1), pp. 81–118.

Pontikes, E. G. & Barnett, W. P. 2015. The persistence of lenient market categories. *Organization Science*, 26, pp. 1415–31.

Porac, J. F., Thomas, H., & Baden-Fuller, C. 1989. Competitive groups as cognitive communities: The case of Scottish knitwear manufacturers. *Journal of Management Studies*, 26(4), pp. 397–416.

Porac, J. F., Thomas, H., Wilson, F., Paton, D., & Kanfer, A. 1995. Rivalry and the industry model of Scottish knitwear producers. *Administrative Science Quarterly*, 40, 203–27.

Porter, M. E. 1980. *Competitive Strategy*. New York: Free Press.

Porter, M. E. 1996. What is strategy? *Harvard Business Review*, 74(6), pp. 61–78.

Posner, M. I. & Keele, S. W. 1968. On the genesis of abstract ideas. *Journal of Experimental Psychology*, 77(3, Pt.1), pp. 353–63.

Powell, T. C. 1992. Organizational alignment as competitive advantage. *Strategic Management Journal*, 13(2): 119–34.

Prato, M., Kypraios, E., Ertug, G., & Lee, Y. G. 2019. Middle-status conformity revisited: The interplay between achieved and ascribed status. *Academy of Management Journal*, 62, pp. 1003–27.

Raffaelli, R. 2019. Technology reemergence: Creating new value for old technologies in Swiss mechanical watchmaking, 1970–2008. *Administrative Science Quarterly*, 64(3), pp. 576–618.

Ragin, C. C. 2000. *Fuzzy-Set Social Science*. Chicago: University of Chicago Press.

Ragin, C. C. 2008. *Redesigning Social Inquiry: Fuzzy Sets and Beyond*. Chicago: University of Chicago Press.

Rao, H. 1994. The social construction of reputation: Certification contests, legitimation, and the survival of organizations in the American automobile industry: 1895–1912. *Strategic Management Journal*, 15(S1), pp. 29–44.

Rao, H., Monin, P., & Durand, R. 2003. Institutional change in Toque Ville: Nouvelle cuisine as an identity movement in French gastronomy. *American Journal of Sociology*, 108, pp. 795–843.

Rao, H., Monin, P., & Durand, R. 2005. Border crossing: Bricolage and the erosion of categorical boundaries in French gastronomy. *American Sociological Review*, 70(6), pp. 968–91.

Rao, H., Morrill, C., & Zald, M. N. 2000. Power plays: How social movements and collective action create new organizational forms. *Research in Organizational Behavior*, 22, pp. 237–81.

Reed, K. 2006. The Elder Scrolls IV: Oblivion. www.eurogamer.net/articles/r_oblivion_x360. Accessed August 23, 2020.

Rosa, J. A., Porac, J. F., Runser-Spanjol, J., & Saxon, M. S. 1999. Sociocognitive dynamics in a product market. *Journal of Marketing*, 63 (4_suppl1), pp. 64–77.

Rosch, E. & Mervis, C. B. 1975. Family resemblances: Studies in the internal structure of categories. *Cognitive Psychology*, 7(4), pp. 573–605.

Ruef, M. & Patterson, K. 2009. Credit and classification: The impact of industry boundaries in nineteenth-century America. *Administrative Science Quarterly*, 54(3), pp. 486–520.

Salomon, R. & Wu, Z. 2012. Institutional distance and local isomorphism strategy. *Journal of International Business Studies*, 43(4), pp. 343–67.

Santos, F. M. & Eisenhardt, K. M. 2009. Constructing markets and shaping boundaries: Entrepreneurial power in nascent fields. *Academy of Management Journal*, 52(4), pp. 643–71.

Saxenian, A. 1994. *Regional Advantage: Culture and Competition in Silicon Valley and Route 128*. Cambridge, MA: Harvard University Press.

Scott W. R. 2001. *Institutions and Organizations* (2nd ed.). Thousand Oaks, CA: Sage Publications.

Semadeni, M. 2006. Minding your distance: How management consulting firms use service marks to position competitively. *Strategic Management Journal*, 27, pp. 169–87.

Sewell, W. 1992. A theory of structure: Duality, agency, and transformation. *American Journal of Sociology*, 98, pp. 1–29.

Siggelkow, N. 2002. Evolution toward fit. *Administrative Science Quarterly*, 47 (1), pp. 125–59.

Simons, T. & Ingram, P. 2004. An ecology of ideology: Theory and evidence from four populations. *Industrial and Corporate Change*, 13(1), pp. 33–59.

Simsek, Z. 2009. Organizational ambidexterity: Towards a multilevel understanding. *Journal of Management Studies*, 46(4), pp. 597–624.

Smith, E. B. & Chae, H. 2016. "We do what we must, and call it the best names": Can deliberate names offset the consequences of organizational atypicality? *Strategic Management Journal*, 37(6): 1021–33.

Smith, E. R. & Zarate, M. A. 1992. Exemplar-based model of social judgment. *Psychological Review*, 99(1), pp. 3–21.

Smith, W. K. & Besharov, M. L. 2019. Bowing before dual gods: How structured flexibility sustains organizational hybridity. *Administrative Science Quarterly*, 64(1): 1–44.

Smith, W. K., Binns, A., & Tushman, M. L. 2010. Complex business models: Managing strategic paradoxes simultaneously. *Long Range Planning*, 43(2), pp. 448–61.

Smith, W. K., Jarzabkowski, P., Lewis, M. W., & Langley, A. 2017. *The Oxford Handbook of Organizational Paradox*. Oxford: Oxford University Press.

Smith, W. K. & Lewis, M. W. 2011. Toward a theory of paradox: A dynamic equilibrium model of organizing. *Academy of Management Review*, 36(2), pp. 381–403.

Snihur, Y., Thomas, L. D. W., & Burgelman, R. A. 2018. An ecosystem-level process model of business model disruption: The disruptor's gambit. *Journal of Management Studies*, 55(7), pp. 1278–316.

Sonenshein, S. 2014. How organizations foster the creative use of resources. *Academy of Management Journal*, 57(3), pp. 814–48.

Souza, G. C., Bayus, B. L., & Wagner, H. M. 2004. New-product strategy and industry clockspeed. *Management Science*, 50(4), pp. 537–49.

Stapel, D. A. & Marx, D. M. 2007. Distinctiveness is key: How different types of self-other similarity moderate social comparison effects. *Personality and Social Psychology Bulletin*, 33(3), pp. 439–48.

Stinchcombe, A. L. 1965. Social structure and organizations. In: G. M. J. (ed.) *Handbook of Organizations*. Chicago: Rand McNally, pp. 142–93.

Suarez, F. F. & Lanzolla, G. 2007. The role of environmental dynamics in building a first mover advantage theory. *Academy of Management Review*, 32 (2), pp. 377–92.

Suchman, M. C. 1995. Managing legitimacy: Strategic and institutional approaches. *Academy of Management Review*, 20(3), pp. 571–610.

Suddaby, R. & Greenwood, R. 2005. Rhetorical strategies of legitimacy. *Administrative Science Quarterly*, 50, 35–67.

Swidler, A. 1986. Culture in action: Symbols and strategies. *American Sociological Review*, pp. 273–86.

Syakhroza, M. A., Paolella, L., & Munir, K. 2019. Holier than thou? Identity buffers and adoption of controversial practices in the Islamic banking category. *Academy of Management Journal*, 62(4), pp. 1252–77.

Taeuscher, K., Bouncken, R. B., & Pesch, R. 2021. Gaining legitimacy by being different: Optimal distinctiveness in crowdfunding platforms. *Academy of Management Journal*, 64(1), pp. 149–79.

Taeuscher, K. & Rothe, H. 2021. Optimal distinctiveness in platform markets: Leveraging complementors as legitimacy buffers. *Strategic Management Journal*, 42(2), pp. 435–61.

Taeuscher, K., Zhao, E. Y., & Lounsbury, M. 2022. Categories and narratives as sources of distinctiveness: Cultural entrepreneurship within and across categories. *Strategic Management Journal*, forthcoming.

Thornton, P. H. & Ocasio, W. 1999. Institutional logics and the historical contingency of power in organizations: Executive succession in the higher education publishing industry, 1958–1990. *American Journal of Sociology*, 105(3), pp. 801–43.

Thornton, P. H., Ocasio, W., & Lounsbury, M. 2012. *The Institutional Logics Perspective: Foundations, Research, and Theoretical Elaboration*. Oxford: Oxford University Press.

Tolbert, P. S. & Zucker, L. G. 1983. Institutional sources of change in the formal structure of organizations: The diffusion of civil service reform, 1880–1935. *Administrative Science Quarterly*, 28, 22–39.

Tracey, P., Dalpiaz, E., & Phillips, N. 2018. Fish out of water: Translation, legitimation, and new venture creation. *Academy of Management Journal*, 61, pp. 1627–66.

Tushman, M. L. & O'Reilly, C. A. 1996. Ambidextrous organizations: Managing evolutionary and revolutionary change. *California Management Review*, 38(4), pp. 8–29.

Vergne, J. P. 2012. Stigmatized categories and public disapproval of organizations: A mixed-methods study of the global arms industry, 1996–2007. *Academy of Management Journal*, 55(5), pp. 1027–52.

Vergne, J. P. & Wry, T. 2014. Categorizing categorization research: Review, integration, and future directions. *Journal of Management Studies*, 51(1), pp. 56–94.

Verhaal, J. C., Khessina, O., & Dobrev, S. 2015. Oppositional product names, organizational identity, and product appeal. *Organization Science*, 26(5), pp. 1466–84.

Wernerfelt, B. 1984. A resource-based view of the firm. *Strategic management Journal*, 5(2), pp. 171–80.

Westphal, J. D. & Clement, M. B. 2008. Sociopolitical dynamics in relations between top managers and security analysts: Favor rendering, reciprocity, and analyst stock recommendations. *Academy of Management Journal*, 51(5), pp. 873–97.

White, H. C. 1981. Where do markets come from? *American Journal of Sociology*, 87, pp. 517–47.

Wolfolds, S. E. & Siegel, J. 2019. Misaccounting for endogeneity: The peril of relying on the Heckman two-step method without a valid instrument. *Strategic Management Journal*, 40, pp. 432–62.

Wry, T. & Zhao, E. Y. 2018. Taking trade-offs seriously: Examining the contextually contingent relationship between social outreach intensity and financial sustainability in global microfinance. *Organization Science*, 29(3), pp. 507–28.

Wry, T., Cobb, J. A., & Aldrich, H. E. 2013. More than a metaphor: Assessing the historical legacy of resource dependence and its contemporary promise as a theory of environmental complexity. *Academy of Management Annals*, 7(1), pp. 441–88.

Wry, T., Lounsbury, M., & Glynn, M. A. 2011. Legitimating nascent collective identities: Coordinating cultural entrepreneurship. *Organization science*, 22(2), pp. 449–463.

Wry, T., Lounsbury, M., & Jennings, P. D. 2014. Hybrid vigor: Securing venture capital by spanning categories in nanotechnology. *Academy of Management Journal*, 57(5), pp. 1309–33.

Wu, Z. & Salomon, R. 2016. Does imitation reduce the liability of foreignness? Linking distance, isomorphism, and performance. *Strategic Management Journal*, 37(12), pp. 2441–62.

Younger, S. & Fisher, G. 2020. The exemplar enigma: New venture image formation in an emergent organizational category. *Journal of Business Venturing*, 35(1), 105897.

Zajac, E. J. & Westphal, J. D. 1994. The costs and benefits of managerial incentives and monitoring in large US corporations: When is more not better? *Strategic Management Journal*, 15(S1), pp. 121–42.

Zhang, Y., Wang, H., & Zhou, X. 2020. Dare to be different? Conformity versus differentiation in corporate social activities of Chinese firms and market responses. *Academy of Management Journal*, 63(3), pp. 717–42.

Zhao, E. Y., Fisher, G., Lounsbury, M., & Miller, D. 2017. Optimal distinctiveness: Broadening the interface between institutional theory and strategic management. *Strategic Management Journal*, 38, pp. 93–113.

Zhao, E. Y. & Glynn, M. A. 2022. Optimal distinctiveness: On being the same and different. *Organization Theory*, forthcoming.

Zhao, E. Y., Ishihara, M., & Jennings, P. D. 2020. Strategic entrepreneurship's dynamic tensions: Converging (diverging) effects of experience and networks on market entry timing and entrant performance. *Journal of Business Venturing*, 35(2), 105933.

Zhao, E. Y., Ishihara, M., Jennings, P. D., & Lounsbury, M. 2018. Optimal distinctiveness in the console video game industry: An exemplar-based model of proto-category evolution. *Organization Science*, 29(4), pp. 588–611.

Zhao, E. Y., Ishihara, M., & Lounsbury, M. 2013. Overcoming the illegitimacy discount: Cultural entrepreneurship in the US feature film industry. *Organization Studies*, 34(12), pp. 1747–76.

Zhao, E. Y. & Lounsbury, M. 2016. An institutional logics approach to social entrepreneurship: Market logic, religious diversity, and resource acquisition by microfinance organizations. *Journal of Business Venturing*, 31(6), pp. 643–62.

Zhao, E. Y. & Wry, T. 2016. Not all inequality is equal: Deconstructing the societal logic of patriarchy to understand microfinance lending to women. *Academy of Management Journal*, 59(6), pp. 1994–2020.

Ziller, R. C. 1964. Individuation and socialization: A theory of assimilation in large organizations. *Human Relations*, 17(4), pp. 341–60.

Zimmerman, M. A. & Zeitz, G. J. 2002. Beyond survival: Achieving new venture growth by building legitimacy. *Academy of Management Review*, 27(3), pp. 414–31.

Zott, C. & Amit, R. 2007. Business model design and the performance of entrepreneurial firms. *Organization Science*, 18(2), pp. 181–99.

Zott, C. & Huy, Q. N. 2007. How entrepreneurs use symbolic management to acquire resources. *Administrative Science Quarterly*, 52(1), pp. 70–105.

Zuckerman, E. W. 1999. The categorical imperative: Securities analysts and the illegitimacy discount. *American Journal of Sociology*, 104(5), pp. 1398–438.

Zuckerman, E. W. 2016. Optimal distinctiveness revisited: An integrative framework for understanding the balance between differentiation and conformity in individual and organizational identities. In Pratt, M. G. et al. (eds.). *Oxford Handbook on Organizational Identity*, Oxford: Oxford University Press, pp. 183–99.

Zuzul, T. & Tripsas, M. 2020. Start-up inertia versus flexibility: The role of founder identity in a nascent industry. *Administrative Science Quarterly*, 65 (2), pp. 395–433.

Acknowledgements

I would like to thank Royston Greenwood and Nelson Phillips for their encouragement and support in the production of this Element. I consider writing this Element as a great opportunity to take stock of research on optimal distinctiveness, reflect on major milestones scholars have collectively achieved, and flesh out an orienting framework to guide the burgeoning conversation on this theory. Various scholars have done pioneering work in this space and significantly influenced my thinking and intellectual development. Some of them generously allocated time to read and comment on earlier drafts of this Element, which helped to clarify and enrich my arguments. I list them here in alphabetical order and thank them sincerely: Gino Cattani, Ming-Jer Chen, David Deephouse, Rudy Durand, Kathy Eisenhardt, Peer Fiss, Mary Ann Glynn, Mike Lounsbury, Wendy Smith, and Paul Tracey. I have also received valuable feedback from inspiring scholars, such as Matthew Barlow, Greg Fisher, Richard Haans, Jade Lo, Majid Majzoubi, Evelyn Micelotta, Lionel Paolella, Eunice Rhee, Karl Taeuscher, J. Cameron Verhaal, and Shannon Younger, whose contributions continue to push the frontier of optimal distinctiveness research. Finally, I thank the two anonymous reviewers who provided very valuable and constructive comments which helped further sharpen my ideas.

Organization Theory

Nelson Phillips
Imperial College London

Nelson Phillips is the Abu Dhabi Chamber Professor of Strategy and Innovation at Imperial College London. His research interests include organization theory, technology strategy, innovation, and entrepreneurship, often studied from an institutional theory perspective.

Royston Greenwood
University of Alberta

Royston Greenwood is the Telus Professor of Strategic Management at the University of Alberta, a visiting professor at the University of Cambridge, and a visiting professor at the University of Edinburgh. His research interests include organizational change and professional misconduct.

Advisory Board

Paul Adler *USC*
Mats Alvesson *Lund University*
Steve Barley *University of Santa Barbara*
Jean Bartunek *Boston College*
Paul Hirsch *Northwestern University*
Ann Langley *HEC Montreal*
Renate Meyer *WU Vienna*
Danny Miller *HEC Montreal*
Mike Tushman *Harvard University*
Andrew Van de Ven *University of Minnesota*

About the Series

Organization theory covers many different approaches to understanding organizations. Its focus is on what constitutes the how and why of organizations and organizing, bringing understanding of organizations in a holistic way. The purpose of *Elements in Organization Theory* is to systematize and contribute to our understanding of organizations.

Cambridge Elements ≡

Organization Theory

Elements in the Series